Quantitative Methods

Erratum to bottom of p.166:

By looking at the expected values of each of the three alternatives, decide which one Mrs Mandel should choose.

Quantitative Methods
A Business Perspective

Diana Bedward

Deputy Dean and Head of the Department of Human Resource Management at the Luton Business School, University of Luton

BUTTERWORTH
HEINEMANN

OXFORD AUCKLAND BOSTON JOHANNESBURG MELBOURNE NEW DELHI

Butterworth-Heinemann
Linacre House, Jordan Hill, Oxford OX2 8DP
225 Wildwood Avenue, Woburn, MA 01801-2041
A division of Reed Educational and Professional Publishing Ltd

A member of the Reed Elsevier plc group

First published 1999

British Library Cataloguing in Publication Data
Bedward, Diana
   Quantitative methods: A Business Perspective
   1. Industrial management – Mathematical models 2. Industrial
   management – Examinations – Study guides
   I. Title
658'.00151

ISBN 0 7506 4093 6

Typeset by Avocet Typeset, Brill, Aylesbury, Bucks
Printed and Bound in Great Britain by Martins the Printers Ltd,
Berwick Upon Tweed

Contents

Preface   ix
Acknowledgements   xi
Introduction   xiii

Chapter 1 The toolkit   1
Handling numbers   2
Decimals   5
Rounding and significant figures   8
Percentages and proportions   9
Powers   13
Representation of business situations   15
Graphs   17
A straight line – a special case   20

Chapter 2 Financial Mathematics   24
Progressions   25
  Arithmetic progressions   26
  Geometric progressions   28
Present value   31
  Net present values   34
Index numbers   36
  Price relative index numbers   37
  Base weighting   39
  Current weighting   42
  'Removing' the effects of inflation   44

Chapter 3 Collecting business information   49
Classification of data   51
  Qualitative data   51
  Quantitative data   51
  Descriptive classes   51
  Ordered classes   52
Rankings   52
Measurements   54

Discrete variables	54
Continuous variables	54
Collecting data	55
Secondary data	55
Primary data	56
Populations and samples	57
Simple random sampling	58
Stratified sampling	60
Cluster sampling	62
Quota sampling	63
Survey methods	63
Observation	64
Experimentation	64
Questioning	64
Chapter 4 Effective business presentations I	**68**
Tabulation	71
Graphs and charts	75
Bar charts	76
Simple bar chart	76
Multiple bar chart	77
Component bar chart	77
Percentage component bar chart	77
Pie charts	79
Z charts	81
Words of caution	84
Using the different diagrams	87
Chapter 5 Effective business presentations II	**91**
Frequency tables	92
Ungrouped frequency tables	92
Grouped frequency tables	94
Unequal class sizes	99
Cumulative frequency tables	99
Histograms	101
Unequal classes	104
Cumulative frequency curves – ogives	106
Chapter 6 Business analysis	**113**
Measures of location	114
The median	114
Finding the median from a simple frequency table	115
Finding the median from a grouped frequency table	116

The mode   119
The arithmetic mean (or simply just the mean)   119
    Finding the mean from a frequency table   120
    Finding the mean from a grouped frequency table   122
Measures of variation   128
    The range   128
    Interquartile range   129
    Standard deviation   131
        Standard deviation for grouped data   134
        Finding the standard deviation from a grouped
        frequency table   136

Chapter 7 Uncertainty in decision making I   **145**
Probability   146
Combining probabilities   150
    The 'OR' rule   150
    The 'AND' rule   151
    Combining probabilities when the events are not
    mutually exclusive   155
Probability trees   157
Expected values   159

Chapter 8 Uncertainty in decision making II   **167**
The normal distribution curve   170
The standard normal distribution   173
    Use of standard normal tables   173
    Conversion to a standard normal distribution   177

Chapter 9 Linear relationships in business   **190**
Linear relationships between two variables   191
Fitting the line   196
    Calculating the least squares regression line   197
The correlation coefficient   203
    A few words of caution   209
Rank correlation   209
    Spearman's rank correlation   209

Chapter 10 Fundamentals of business forecasting   **221**
Long-term forecasting   223
Short-term forecasting   225
Estimating trend using moving averages   227
Estimating the seasonal variation   232
Forecasting   234

Other forecasting models   240

Integrating case studies   **244**
Short answers   **250**
Glossary of terms   **273**
Appendix A   **275**
Appendix B   **277**

Index   279

Preface

Most undergraduate and HND courses in business and management include quantitative methods, in some form or other, in their first year.

Quantitative Methods – A Business Perspective has been written for those first year business studies students who are not mathematicians, yet need to understand and apply quantitative methods to business situations. It may also appeal to first year IPD, DMS and MBA students who are returning to study after a few years spent establishing their careers.

In the book many topics are explored using a case study approach, enabling the reader to understand the need for the techniques, before being confronted with them. The style is friendly, and takes the reader steadily through each topic, using examples and activities to reinforce the learning. Where possible, mathematical proofs are avoided. Often, students find the use of mathematical symbols confusing so there is a quick reference glossary at the back of the book.

The reader is encouraged to carry out the analyses using a spreadsheet package, however, this is not essential, a calculator will suffice.

Each chapter concludes with a self-assessment, covering multiple choice questions, exercises and case studies. Since most business problems are not confined to a single quantitative topic, there are further integrating case studies at the end of the book.

Acknowledgements

I would like to express my thanks to my colleagues at the University of Luton who have encouraged me in the compilation of this book. In particular to Christine Rexworthy, who read the entire book several times, noticing and correcting misprints and inconsistencies in the text, and suggesting modifications which always improved the clarity. I am also grateful to my students who have worked through the examples, case studies and activities.

I also acknowledge the assistance of the organizations that have kindly provided relevant material: Macmillan Press Ltd, London and Basingstoke, and J. Murdock and J.A. Murdock for the use of Tables 3 and 4 from *Statistical Tables for Science, Engineering, Management and Business Studies* (4th Edition); The Guardian Newspaper for the use of the table '*Anecdotal Indicators of Recession*'; Management Publications Ltd, The Institute of Management and Loughborough Business School. Whilst every effort has been made to identify the specific sources of such material in order to request permission for their use, in some instances this may not have been possible and I apologize for any failure in this regard.

Introduction

Welcome to *Quantitative Methods – A Business Perspective.* I hope you find it a useful and readable text, or at least as readable as a quantitative text can be! Please take a few minutes to read this introduction, as I hope it will explain the approach that I have used in the book.

Do not worry if it has been a while since you last studied a numerical subject, particularly if you gave it up in delight because you found it difficult. The first chapter is designed to refresh your memory. It covers the mathematical foundation needed for you to cope with the rest of the book. Even if you are fairly numerate, I suggest that you try the self-assessments at the start of each section in Chapter 1, just to re-assure yourself.

If you come across any unfamiliar symbol – and numerate subjects do use a lot of symbols – there is a glossary at the back of the book, designed to help. Simply remember that the symbols are just a form of shorthand.

Each chapter starts with a set of aims, which you should have achieved by the time you reach the end of the chapter. I try and set the scene in the introduction to each chapter.

The key to success in quantitative methods is to take each topic slowly, make sure you understand each one before moving onto the next. You will find that the topics build on each other, so if you do not understand one particular section try it again, reworking the examples. Don't just carry on hoping that inspiration will come, you will only succeed in confusing yourself. You may find it helps to spend half an hour each day working on your current topic, rather than several hours all at once.

There is really no substitute for practice and the book contains lots of activities and worked examples, and each chapter ends with a self-assessment. You should aim to complete them all. However, much of the work can be done using a calculator or the spreadsheet package on your computer. The accompanying disk uses Microsoft Excel. **Before you start using the disk copy it and put the original away in a safe place**. When you open the workbook you will find that there are several worksheets relating to each chapter (except for

Chapters 1 and 3). The first worksheet is empty so that you can try the activities and self-assessments by yourself, without any help. The second worksheet has hints on how to solve the activities, using any preprogrammed functions, and the skeleton of the solution set up for you to complete. All exercises that involve calculations will be on the disk. This will be shown by an icon ▣ at the beginning of the exercise.

Of course, you do not need access to a computer to succeed: a calculator, a pencil rather than pen (so that you can erase your mistakes) and graph paper are sufficient. The short answers to the activities and self-assessments are at the back of the book.

Each chapter has a set of worked examples. You should work through them, checking that you understand each step, rather than skipping over them. You may find that you have to work out some of the calculations in greater detail than shown.

You will notice that many of the chapters, and several of the case studies, cover different ways of presenting data. The ability to clearly present data in either a written report or in a presentation is a valuable skill that you will probably find useful in the future.

Good luck.

Chapter 1

The toolkit

The aims of this chapter are to revise the basic mathematical tools, which form the foundation for all the techniques and business applications covered later in this book.

By the end of this chapter you will have reinforced your understanding of:

Aims

- handling numbers: positive, negative, decimals
- rounding numbers to a given number of decimal places or significant figures
- the calculation of percentages and proportions
- the use and arithmetic of powers
- the use of mathematical expressions to represent business situations
- the construction of graphs.

Key Concepts

- numbers
- variables
- decimals
- rounding
- percentages

- proportions
- powers
- equations
- graphs

Introduction

This chapter provides a refresher coverage of the basic mathematical toolkit, which underpins business quantitative methods. You will be familiar with most of the techniques already, probably from school or college. Some may be so familiar to you that you feel it unnecessary to revise them. Others are a distant memory, long forgotten, or may not have seemed important at the time. To guide you in deciding which topics you should revise, there is a short self-assessment at the start of each section. Try working through these without referring to the text. If you get all the answers right, then you can skip that section. (The answers are given at the back of the book.)

After working through a section, you will find another self-assessment, designed to enable you to check on your progress. As practice really is essential if you are to become familiar with these topics, you could also re-try the self-assessment at the start of the section. Hopefully, you will get more right at the second attempt.

In some of the later chapters you may come across unfamiliar symbols. If this is the case then you should refer to the glossary at the back of the book. Symbols are really a form of shorthand, and save us having to write expressions out in full.

Handling numbers

Self-assessment 1.1

Self Assessments

Answer the questions below as best you can, without using a calculator.

1 $18 + 3 - 7$
2 $54 - 67 \times 2$
3 $-121 - 47$
4 $-56 \div 7$
5 $(-5) \times (8 - 4)$

Numbers are the language of our mathematical toolkit. Quantitative methods use numbers to represent business situations, to determine solutions to business problems, and as an aid in presenting information to business colleagues. Do not worry if you are not confident about working with numbers at this stage: you are not alone. Many managers cannot easily understand and assimilate numerical information.

Numbers can be:

- positive or negative
- whole (integer) or decimals.

You are probably confident working with positive *integers* (whole numbers), and even decimals but less so with negative numbers. The minus sign always seems to get in the way. Even calculators can have trouble coping with them!

But you can think of negative numbers as simply a mirror image of their positive counterpart, with zero acting as the mirror in the middle.

Try listing the integers 0 to 5 on a line. The negative numbers from –5 to 0 are a mirror image of these:

- Integers 0 to 5

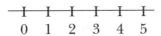

- Negative integers –5 to 0

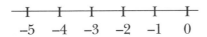

- Then we can put the two lines of numbers together, to show how the image works

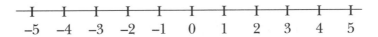

The gaps between the integers are filled with the decimal numbers.

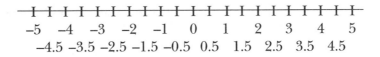

Addition and subtraction are ways of moving up and down the line.

- **Adding** 3 to 6 is simply moving 3 points **up** from 6 to 9
- **Subtracting** 2 from 8 is moving 2 points **down** from 8 to 6

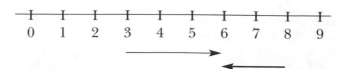

- **Adding** 3 to –6 is moving 3 points **up** from –6 to –3
- **Subtracting** 2 from –5 is moving 2 points **down** from –5 to –7, this is also the same as adding –2 to –5

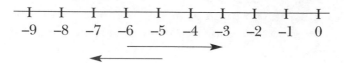

Multiplying and dividing negative numbers or a combination of positive and negative numbers can also cause difficulty. There are three basic rules that always apply:

1 Two positive numbers multiplied together or divided by each other always give a POSITIVE number.
2 Two negative numbers multiplied together or divided by each other always give a POSITIVE number.
3 One positive and one negative number multiplied together or divided by each other always give a NEGATIVE number.

For example:

1   $(-3) \times (-6) = +18$
2   $(-2) \times 5 = -10$
3   $(-12) \div (-2) = +6$

Sometimes / is used instead of ÷, e.g.

$8/(-4) = -2$

One final point in this section is that it is important to perform calculations in the right order:

- Work out the inside of any brackets first.
- Then do any multiplication and division.
- Lastly add and subtract.

For example:

$3 + 6 \times (7 - 4)$

1 Working out the brackets

$$= 3 + 6 \times 3$$

2 Multipying

$$= 3 + 18$$

3 Finally adding

$$= 21$$

You will need to remember these rules apply even when using a simple pocket calculator.

There are occasions when we might not actually know the number, or we may wish to make a general statement that applies to a range of numbers. Then, it is common practice to replace this unknown number, by a letter, often x.

This letter is called a **variable** as its values can vary.

Many general mathematical rules use variables instead of numbers, leaving it to us to replace the variables by actual numbers.

Self-assessment 1.2

Answer the questions below, without using a calculator.

1   $15 + 3 - 27$
2   $24 - 7 \times (2 + 5)$
3   $-120/-30$
4   $56 \div (-8)$
5   $(-5) \times (18-24)$

Decimals

Self-assessment 1.3

Answer the questions below as best you can, without using a calculator.

1   $0.5 + 0.3$

2   8.4 − 7.3
3   0.6 × 0.01
4   0.25/0.1
5   3.6 × 0.3 × 0.33
6   6.2/(−0.2)

As we noted earlier decimal numbers fill in the gaps between the integers on our line of numbers. If you divide the gap between any two integers into 10 equal parts, these give the position of the decimals.

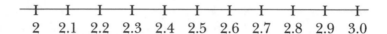

2   2.1   2.2   2.3   2.4   2.5   2.6   2.7   2.8   2.9   3.0

The new gaps can also be divided into ten equal parts and these give the **second decimal places**:

- 2.01, 2.02, 2.03, 2.04, 2.05, 2.06, 2.07, 2.08, 2.09
- 2.11, 2.12, 2.13, 2.14, 2.15, 2.16, 2.17, 2.18, 2.19
- 2.21, 2.22, 2.13, 2.14, 2.15, 2.16, 2.17, 2.18, 2.29

etc.

Addition and subtraction of decimals follow the same processes as for integers. But bear in mind to line up the decimal points.

Multiplication and division are more likely to cause problems, as the decimal point can easily end up in the wrong place, making the answer wrong by several orders of magnitude.

When multiplying, the number of decimal places in the answer is the *total* number of decimal places in the numbers being multiplied.

For example:

- 2.1 × 3.5 × 1.01 has a total of four numbers after the decimal points, so the answer will have four numbers after the decimal point.
- 2.1 × 3.5 × 1.01 = 7.4235
- 3.3 × 0.01 has three numbers after the decimal points so the answer will be 0.033.
- 3.3 × 0.001 has four numbers giving 0.0033
- 1000 × 0.001 has three numbers giving 1.000

Even if you are doing your calculations using a calculator or a computer, it is wise to check that you have the expected number of digits behind the decimal point. Such a simple check can ensure that the size of the answer is of the size expected. If the answer is several orders of magnitude bigger, or smaller, than expected you should check that the decimal points in the data were entered correctly.

Division of decimals is slightly more complicated. But there is a little trick that makes the operation simpler. That is to change the denominator, or the divisor, into an integer by moving the decimal point. Count the number of places that you have to move the decimal point to make the denominator an integer, then move the decimal point of the numerator exactly the same number of places.

For example $12.55 \div 0.5$

Here the divisor, 0.5, has one number behind the decimal point:

● move the decimal point of 0.5 one place to the right, giving 5

then

● move the decimal point of 12.55 one place to the right.

This gives $125.5 \div 5 = 25.1$

By moving the decimal point one, or two, places to the right we are actually multiplying **both** the numerator and the denominator, by 10, or 100. The overall answer is unchanged, but easier to calculate.

Self-assessment 1.4

Answer the questions below, without using a calculator. Remember that the topics you learnt in the first section also apply to decimals.

1 $0.8 + 0.73$
2 $15.44 - 7.12$
3 6×0.01
4 $0.2/0.1$
5 $5.2/(-0.2)$
6 $-8.4/0.04$

Rounding and significant figures

Self-assessment 1.5

Round the following figures to the required number of decimal places:

1 2.567 to two decimal places
2 3.4561 to three decimal places
3 89.359 to one decimal place

Express the following to the stated number of significant figures:

4 2846.7 to four significant figures
5 3756 to two significant figures
6 194,100 to three significant figures

When you use your calculator or a spreadsheet on your computer to calculate certain values, you often find that the answer can have eight or nine numbers after the decimal point – far more than you are really interested in. It is useful to be able to reduce these by **rounding to a given number of decimal places**.

There is no hard and fast rule for determining how many decimal places would be appropriate in a particular set of circumstances. It often depends on the number of decimal places in the original data. Usually, if the original data is in £s, then we really only need two decimal places, the pence, in our final answer.

The general rule for rounding is:

● 5 and above are rounded up

and

● below 5 are rounded down

This means that, if we want to express 3.5652 to two decimal places, it is **rounded up** to give 3.57. Alternatively, 3.5642 rounded to two decimal places, is **rounded down** to give 3.56.

Significant figures are often used when dealing with very large numbers, particularly where there is a degree of doubt about the accuracy of the last few digits.

For example, if the population of a town is thought to be 1 173 561 then this can be expressed as:

1 174 000 to four significant figures

or

1 170 000 to three significant figures.

Self-assessment 1.6

Round the following figures to the required number of decimal places:

1   22.157 to two decimal places
2   0.0233 to three decimal places
3   8.449 to one decimal place

Express the following to the stated number of significant figures:

4   1 852 846.7 to four significant figures
5   194 100 to three significant figures
6   687 533 to two significant figures

Percentages and proportions

Self-assessment 1.7

Find the following percentages:

1   25 out of 800
2   7.5 out of 225
3   6 out of 90

Find:

4   10 per cent of 50
5   25 per cent of 625
6   30 per cent of 900
7   An item, which cost £2, is to be increased in price by 10 per cent. What is the new price?

8 Value Added Tax (VAT) is applied at a rate of 17.5 per cent. What is the price inclusive of VAT, if an item costs £60 before VAT is added?

Find the following proportions:

9 3 out of 6
10 7 out of 21
11 15 out of 450

Percentages are always based on 100: 100 items, 100 people, £100 etc.

The basic rule for calculating a percentage is:

To find what percent one number is of another number

1 Divide the first number by the second number
2 Then multiply the answer by 100

Or, using variables:

To find what percent *x* is of *y*

1 Divide the *x* by *y*
2 Then multiply the answer by 100

Imagine we have a group of 750 employees, of whom 350 are women. The percentage of women, will be the number of women among every 100 employees.

$$\text{Percentage of women} = \frac{\text{Number of women}}{\text{Number of employees}} \times 100$$

$$= \frac{350}{750} \times 100$$

$$= 46.67 \text{ per cent to two decimal places}$$

Percentages are particularly useful for comparing characteristics of different sized groups, as each group is represented by 100.

For example, if our employees work two different shifts: Group A, the early shift has 300 employees and Group B, the late shift has 450 employees. There are 120 women in Group A, and 230 in Group B.

As the two shifts are different sizes, comparison between them is difficult, unless we use percentages.

Percentage of women in Group A =
$$\frac{\text{Number of women in Group A}}{\text{Number of employees in Group A}} \times 100$$

$$= \frac{120}{300} \times 100$$

$$= 40 \text{ per cent}$$

Percentage of women in Group B =
$$\frac{\text{Number of women in Group B}}{\text{Number of employees in Group B}} \times 100$$

$$= \frac{230}{450} \times 100$$

$$= 51.11 \text{ per cent to two decimal places}$$

Proportions are based on a similar idea, but here instead of using a figure of 100, the total used is 1.

Remember

The basic rule for calculating a proportion is:

To find what proportion one number (x) is of another number (y)

● Divide the first number by the second number (x/y)

For example, to calculate the proportion of women employed, divide the number of women by the total number of employees.

● So the proportion of women employees is $350/750 = 0.47$ (to two decimal places)

● The proportion in Group A is 120/300 = 0.4
● The proportion in Group B is 230/450 = 0.51 (to two decimal places)

There are occasions when the percentage is known, and we need to find how many or how much this actually represents. For instance if a restaurant adds a 10 per cent service charge to our bill, it is useful to be able to calculate how much this will be.

Remember

The rule for finding the actual amount that a percentage represents is:

1 Multiply the number by the percentage
2 Divide by 100

For example, if the food in the restaurant cost £25, the 10 per cent service charge equals:

$$\frac{10 \times 25}{100}$$

= 2.5

= £2.50p

Self-assessment 1.8

Find the following percentages:

1 5 out of 70
2 15 out of 225
3 60 out of 540

Find

4 10 per cent of 550
5 2.5 per cent of 625
6 10 per cent of 850

7   An item, which cost £20, is to be increased in price by 12.5 per cent. What is the new price?

8   Value Added Tax (VAT) is applied at a rate of 17.5 per cent. What is the price inclusive of VAT, if an item costs £78 before VAT is added?

Find the following proportions

9   33 out of 66
10   75 out of 510
11   25 out of 625

Powers

Self-assessment 1.9

Find the values of the following:

1   10^4
2   10^{-2}
3   2^3
4   $\sqrt{16}$
5   $1000^{1/3}$
6   $\sqrt[3]{8}$

A short way of writing $8 \times 8 \times 8$ is to write 8^3, 8 cubed, or 8 to the power 3. The 3 is called the power, it tells us to multiply 8 by itself 3 times.

Similarly 8^5, is 8 to the power of 5, telling us to multiply 8 by itself 5 times.

Many calculators have a button labelled x^y, this will find the value of a number, x, raised to the power y. Of course, we have to enter the values of x and y. A quick way of finding the square of a number with a calculator, is to

● enter the number
● then press the multiplication sign
● then the equals sign.

Similarly all spreadsheets will calculate powers, by using the ^ key. So 8 raised to the power of 5, is entered as 8^5.

Sometimes you will see a number raised to a negative power, such as 16^{-2}.

This is a short way of writing $1/16^2$, or $1/256 = 0.003\ 906\ 2$

A negative power means 1 divided by the amount.

Powers which are expressed as fractions mean take the root of the number.

For example:

$100^{1/2}$ means take the square root of 100 (=10, as 10 has to multiplied by itself to give 100). It can also be written as $\sqrt{100}$. Most calculators have a square root key.

$1000^{1/3}$ means take the cubed root of 1000 (=10, as 10 has to be multiplied by itself 3 times to get 1000).

It can also be written as $\sqrt[3]{1000}$.

Remember

In general:

The *n*th root of a number, *x*, which is written as:

$x^{1/n}$ or $\sqrt[n]{x}$

is the number, which when multiplied by itself *n* times comes to *x*.

As you can, tell this can be difficult to calculate, and thankfully the ^ key on a spreadsheet will find the values for us, provided we put the $1/n$ in a bracket after the ^ sign.

$1000^{1/3}$ is entered into the spreadsheet as $1000^\wedge(1/3)$.

Self-assessment 1.10

Find the values of the following:

1   10^3
2   10^{-1}
3   4^3

4 $^3\sqrt{64}$
5 $10\,000^{1/2}$
6 $^3\sqrt{8}$

Representation of business situations

Self-assessment 1.11

Your employer pays you a monthly salary. Each month £100 is deducted for your pension contributions. You pay tax on the remainder at a rate of 20 per cent. Using G as your gross monthly salary and T as your monthly take home pay, after all deductions, write an equation for calculating your take home pay.

Many business situations can be succinctly described using **variables** and **equations** instead of words. These equations can then be solved, giving a solution to the business problem. The difficulty is not necessarily solving the equations, but developing the equation in the first place. We can often describe a situation in words, but are unable to represent it using variables and equations.

● The first step is to assign a letter to each unknown quantity. These are the variables in our problem.
● Then try and express the relationship between the variables, giving an equation.

For example, a company pays its production staff an hourly rate. We can develop a formula for calculating an individual's weekly wage, which, in words, will be the hourly rate multiplied by the number of hours worked.

● First, give each of the unknowns a letter:
   – The hourly rate = r
   – The number of hours worked in the week = h
   – The weekly wage = w
● Then, using these letters, develop the relationship between them

$w = h \times r$

Let's now work through Self-assessment 1.11 given at the start of this section and reproduced again below. It is slightly more complicated, although the unknowns have already been assigned their letters.

The company that employs you pays you a monthly salary. Each month £100 is deducted for your pension contributions. You pay tax on the remainder at a rate of 20 per cent. Using G as your gross monthly salary and T as your monthly take home pay, after all deductions, write an equation for calculating your take home pay.

1 Gross monthly salary = G
2 Take home pay = T

In the written description, the first thing that happens is that £100 is deducted for pension contribution, so we deduct 100 from the gross salary:

● $G - 100$

Tax is paid on this amount at a rate of 20 per cent

● Tax paid = 20 per cent of $(G - 100) = 0.2 \times (G - 100)$

Putting these together gives the take home pay formula:

● $T = G - 100 - 0.2 \times (G - 100)$

Once we know the actual value of G we can find the actual take home pay.

Self-assessment 1.12

Develop formulae for the following situations:

1 Mr Brown is going shopping in the town centre, five miles away. The bus fare to the town centre is 10p per mile. When he gets there he decides to buy oranges at 15p each, cucumbers at 50p each and 500 g of mince. What is the total cost of the shopping trip?
2 A loaf of bread is made from 500 g of flour, 2 g of yeast and 300 ml of water. The fuel to operate the oven costs 3p per loaf. What is the total cost of making the loaf?

Graphs

Self-assessment 1.13

Plot the following graphs across the suggested ranges:

1 $y = 3 + 2x$ from $x = -3$ to $x = +3$
2 $y = 1 + x - 2x^2$ from $x = -2$ to $x = +2$

Graphs are a good visual way of representing an equation. It is a way of making a dull string of letters and numbers look more meaningful and is relatively easy to achieve now that computer graphics packages are so sophisticated.

A graph starts with two lines, called **axes**, drawn at right angles to each other. The horizontal axis is called the **x-axis** and the vertical the **y-axis**. Both axes are marked out in a scale.

The point where the axes cross is called the **origin**, and corresponds to the values $x = 0$ and $y = 0$ on the scales.

To plot a graph we need to:

● work out a range of points, which lie on the graph
● plot them

and then

● join up the points.

As an example we will draw the graph of the equation:

$y = 2x + x^2 - 15$ between $x = -4$ and $x = +4$

We will calculate a range of points from $x = -4$ to $x = +4$ by constructing a table, which has a column for the values of x, one column for each term in the equation, and one for the resulting value of y. This is shown in Table 1.1. The numbers in the remaining columns are then filled in, as shown in Table 1.2. If you are working out the values on your spreadsheet try using the 'copy' function. Table 1.3 gives the values of x and y for the points that we are going to plot on our graph.

The scale on the x-axis has to go from at least -4 to $+4$, and that on the y-axis must go from at least -15 to $+9$, as these are the range of values of x and y.

Table 1.1 To calculate the points of $y = 2x + x^2 - 15$ between $x = -4$ and $x = +4$

x	2x	x^2	−15	y
−4				
−3				
−2				
−1				
0				
1				
2				
3				
4				

Table 1.2 Values of $y = 2x + x^2 - 15$ between $x = -4$ and $x = +4$

x	2x	x^2	−15	y
−4	−8	16	−15	−7
−3	−6	9	−15	−12
−2	−4	4	−15	−15
−1	−2	1	−15	−16
0	0	0	−15	−15
1	2	1	−15	−12
2	4	4	−15	−7
3	6	9	−15	0
4	8	16	−15	9

Table 1.3 The points to be plotted on the graph

x	y	x	y
−4	−7	1	−12
−3	−12	2	−7
−2	−15	3	0
−1	−16	4	9
0	−15		

We can now plot the graph, as shown in Figure 1.1.

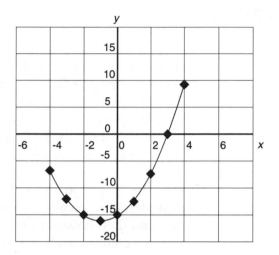

Figure 1.1 The graph of $y = 2x + x^2 - 15$ between $x = -4$ and $x = +4$

You may also like to try plotting the graph using the graph function on your spreadsheet.

- Enter the x and y values given in Table 1.3 onto the spreadsheet.
- Highlight the values.
- Select the chart function.
- Select the xy scatter graphs.
- Choose the most appropriate graph from the set of possibilities – probably one of the line graphs.
- Then follow the instructions which appear on your screen to customize the labels, and headings etc.

Self-assessment 1.14

Plot the following graphs across the suggested ranges:

1   $y = 5 - 2x$ from $x = -4$ to $x = +4$
2   $y = 10 - x - 2x^2$ from $x = -2$ to $x = +2$

A straight line – a special case

Self-assessment 1.15

1. Draw the graph of $y = 10 - 3x$ between $x = -1$ and $x = 4$
2. Draw the graph of $y = -5 + 4x$ between $x = -3$ and $x = 3$
3. In the equation $y = 5 + 6x$, what is the value of the intercept?
4. In the equation $y = 10 - 3x$ what is the value of the slope?
5. In the equation $y = 2 + 10x$, by how much does y increase if the value of x is increased by 1?

Two of the graphs in the self-assessments 1.13 and 1.14 were also both straight-line graphs. In this section we will look at straight-line graphs and their equations in more detail.

The two graphs are shown in Figures 1.2 and 1.3 for reference.

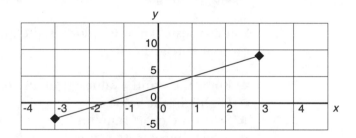

Figure 1.2 Graph of $y = 3 + 2x$

- In Figure 1.2, the graph $y = 3 + 2x$, crosses the y-axis at the point where $y = 3$
- In Figure 1.3, the graph $y = 5 - 2x$ crosses the y-axis where $y = 5$

Both these points occur when $x = 0$, and this point is called the **intercept**.

The graph of $y = 3 + 2x$ slopes upwards, whereas $y = 5 - 2x$ slopes downwards, both with the same gradient or **slope**.

The sign in front of the 'x' term indicates the direction of the slope:

- A plus sign indicates a positive slope, and as x increases so does y
- A minus sign indicates a negative slope, and as x increases y decreases.

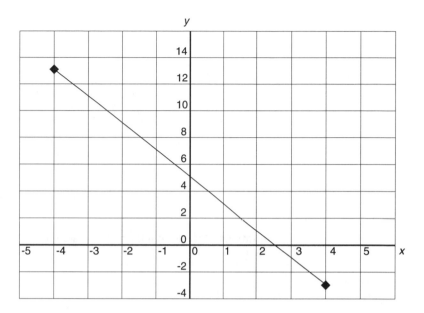

Figure 1.3 Graph of $y = 5 - 2x$

The coefficient of x (i.e. the number x is multiplied by) indicates the rate of increase or decrease in y with x.

You can check this by referring back to the table you produced to calculate the values of y for each value of x.

You will see that for every 1 that x increases:

- y increases by 2, in the calculation for $y = 3 + 2x$, and
- y decreases by 2, in the calculations for $y = 5 - 2x$

The intercept and the slope totally define any straight line. This means that we can express the equation of a straight line in the general form:

$$y = a + bx$$

where:

- a = the intercept
- b = the slope.

The sign of 'b' indicates the direction of the slope.

This is illustrated in Figures 1.4 and 1.5.

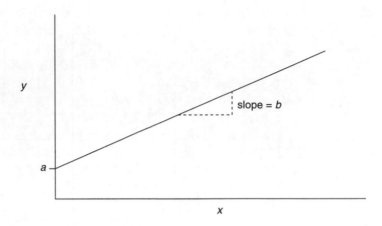

Figure 1.4 The general form of a straight-line graph with a positive slope, $y = a + bx$

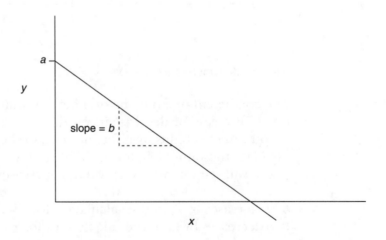

Figure 1.5 The general form of a straight-line graph with a negative slope, $y = a + bx$ when b is negative

Self-assessment 1.16

1 Draw the graph of $y = 12 - 4x$, between $x = -1$ and $x = 4$
2 Draw the graph of $y = -10 + 5x$, between $x = -3$ and $x = 3$
3 In the equation $y = 15 + 7x$, what is the value of the intercept?
4 In the equation $y = 30 - 23x$, what is the value of the slope?
5 In the equation $y = 2 + 5x$, by how much does y increase if the value of x is increased by 1?

Summary

This chapter was designed to refresh your mathematical skills, covering only those techniques that underpin the remainder of the book.

The areas we revised were the manipulation of positive and negative numbers, both integer and decimal. Multiplying and dividing by decimal numbers often causes problems, and answers with a decimal point in the wrong place can cause business solutions to be wrong by orders of magnitude. We should always ask ourselves 'Is this the size of number I was expecting?'. We then looked at rounding and significant figures, as often a computer-generated solution gives us more numbers than we really require.

We revised the methods of calculating percentages and proportions. These figures are often important statistics in business, and used when comparing the characteristics of different sized groups.

You will find the section on powers underpins the next chapter, which covers financial mathematics.

Finally we revised the whole area of equations, and graphs, paying particular attention to the straight-line relationship, which will be important when we consider regression analysis later.

Further reading

Rowe, R.N. (1990). *A Refresher Course in Basic Mathematics*, 2nd edn, DP Publications.
Riley, T. (1990). *A Way With Numbers*, BBC Publications.

Chapter 2
Financial mathematics

The aim of this chapter is to apply certain areas of mathematics, developed in the previous chapter, to business situations.

By the end of this chapter you will be able to:

- recognize and apply arithmetic and geometric progressions to business situations
- calculate simple and compound interest
- calculate the value of depreciation over time
- understand and be able to calculate present values as a method of making investment decisions
- understand the construction and use of index numbers, both base and current weighted.

- arithmetic progressions
- geometric progressions
- simple interest
- compound interest
- depreciation
- present value

- net present value
- index numbers
- General index of retail prices
- Laspeyres price index
- Paasche price index

Introduction

There are many business situations which follow regular patterns: machines depreciate in value from one year to the next, salaries can increase by annual instalments, money is invested and earns interest, loans are repaid etc. Additionally, businesses need to make investment decisions based on sound financial footings. These investment decisions usually depend on current and predicted interest rates.

All these situations can be represented mathematically and use some of the tools developed in the last chapter, so you should be sure that you are happy with these tools before proceeding.

This chapter can only give you a small insight into the field of financial decision making. It is an area where businesses need sound advice from financial experts. It will, however, enable you to communicate with these experts and help you understand more fully their proposals and recommendations.

Case Study

Luciano's is a small family firm specializing in the manufacture of organic ice cream. In five years' time their large commercial freezer will need replacing, and will probably then cost £50,000. The family decides to look at methods of financing the purchase now, rather than waiting until the freezer needs replacing. The options they are considering include:

- Regular savings.
- Investing a sum of money now, which will mature into the amount needed.
- Waiting until the freezer needs replacing, then purchasing a new model.
- Waiting until the freezer needs replacing, then leasing a new model.

In this chapter we will consider these alternatives and the financial implications for Luciano's.

Progressions

These are mathematical models where a variable, usually money or the monetary value of an item, takes a set of different values as time progresses.

● An investment of a sum of money, which attracts regular interest payments, is an example of a variable (money) increasing over time.
● The value of a car, which decreases each year, is a particular example of monetary value decreasing over time.

Arithmetic progressions

In an arithmetic progression the variable increases, or decreases, by a fixed amount during each time period. This fixed amount is called the **common difference**. Examples of arithmetic progressions include:

1 *Simple interest* – A man invests his savings of £2000 at a fixed interest rate of 7 per cent per annum. At the end of each year the interest is sent to him. He puts the interest paid in a biscuit tin in the kitchen.

The yearly interest paid = 7 per cent of £2000

$$= £\frac{7}{100} \times 2000$$

$$= £140$$

So each year he puts £140 in the biscuit tin, and his savings increase by £140 (the common difference).

The total value of his savings will be:

After 1 year = £2000 + 140 = £2140
After 2 years = £2000 + 2 × 140 = £2280
After 3 years = £2000 + 3 × 140 = £2420
And so on.

In general, after n years his savings will be £2000 + n × 140

2 *Linear depreciation* – A machine is bought for £85 000. The company's management accountant assesses its annual depreciation as £7500.

The value of the machine is therefore assessed as being:

After 1 year = £85 000 – 7500 = £77 500
After 2 years = £85 000 – 2 × 7500 = £70 000
After 3 years = £85 000 – 3 × 7500 = £62 500

After n years the value is assessed as being £85 000 – n × 7500
    Here, the common difference is –£7500.
    These two examples lead us to the general format of an arithmetic progression as being:

1 The initial value.
2 The initial value + the common difference.
3 The initial value + 2 × the common difference.
4 The initial value + 3 × the common difference.
5 The initial value + 4 × the common difference.

The nth term = The initial value + $(n – 1)$ × the common difference

Example

A machine, which cost £12 000 when new, is to be linearly depreciated. Its scrap value after eight years will be £2400.

(a) By how much should the value be depreciated each year?
(b) What will be its value after five years?

(a) The initial value of the machine = £12 000
    If d = the annual depreciation = the common difference.
    Then:

    After 1 year the value = £12 000 – d
    After 2 years the value = £12 000 – 2 × d
    The scrap value after 8 years = £2400 = £12 000 – 8 × d

    Or

    2400 = 12 000 – 8 × d
    d = –1200, i.e. the common difference = –£1200

(b) After 1 year the value = £12 000 – 1200
    After 2 years = £12 000 – 2 × 1200
    After 5 years = £12 000 – 5 × 1200 = £12 000 – 6000 =

The Luciano family is considering investing a lump sum now, which will accumulate over the next five years to produce the £50 000 needed for the new freezer. The bank is offering a fixed interest rate of 8 per cent per annum.

Case Study
Exercise 1

Calculate the amount that the Luciano family needs to invest now if they invest it for five years using simple interest at 8 per cent per annum.

Geometric progressions

A geometric progression is a series where the variable increases, or decreases, by multiplying the previous value by a fixed amount. This fixed multiplier is called the **common ratio**. Examples of geometric progressions include:

1 *Compound interest* – This time the man invests his £2000 savings, and leaves the annual interest in the account. Here the investment increases each year:

   After 1 year the savings = £2000 + 7 per cent of 2000 = £2140 (as before)
   After 2 years the savings = £2140 + 7 per cent of 2140 = 2140 + 149.8 = £2289.8
   After 3 years = £2289 + 7 per cent of 2289.8 = 2289.8 + 160.286 = £2450.086

2 *Depreciation by a fixed percentage each year* – A machine costs £45 000, its value is depreciated by 30 per cent each year.

   After 1 year it is worth £45 000 – 30 per cent of £45 000
   = £45 000 – £13 500
   = £31 500
   After 2 years it is worth £31 500 – 30 per cent of £31 500

= £31 500 − £9450
= £22 050
After 3 years it is worth £22 050 − 30 per cent of £22 050
= £22 050 − £6615
= £15 435

And so on.

With geometric progressions the general format is not as easy to see as it was with the arithmetic progressions. However, there is one that we can determine by looking at the example of compound interest in a slightly different way.

The initial amount = £2000
After 1 year it is worth £(2000 + 7 per cent of 2000)
= 2000 + 0.07 × 2000
as both terms have a common factor of 2000 this can be expressed as
= 2000 × (1 + 0.07)

After 2 years it is worth 2000 × (1+0.07) + 7 per cent of 2000 × (1 + 0.07)
= 2000 × (1 + 0.07) + 0.07 × 2000 × (1 + 0.07)
This time there is a common factor of 2000 × (1 + 0.07)
= 2000 × (1+0.07)^2

After 3 years it is worth 2000 × (1+0.07)^3

After n years it will be worth 2000 × (1+0.07)^n

In general, if an amount P, the principal, is invested at an interest rate of i per cent per annum then, after n years it will be worth:

$P(1 + i/100)^n$

Sometimes, compound interest is paid into an account twice a year. Then the amount P, invested at i per cent per annum, attracts an interest rate of 0.5 × i per cent each half year. If the investment is kept for n years, there will be $2n$ payments. The investment will then be worth:

$P(1 + 0.5 × i/100)^{2n}$

An initial value, P, to be depreciated by a rate of i per cent per annum, over n years will be worth:

$$P(1 - i/100)^n$$

Example

A machine, bought new for £20 000, is to be depreciated annually by 10 per cent. What will it be worth:

(a) after six years?
(b) after 10 years?

(a) Initial value = £20 000
   After six years it will be worth:
   £20 000 × $(1 - 0.1)^6$
   = £20 000 × 0.9^6
   = £10 628.82

   The calculation can be easily done using either a calculator with an x^y function, or on a spreadsheet using the ^ key. That is to find 0.9^6 on a spreadsheet enter 0.9^6.

(b) After 10 years it will be worth:
   £20 000 × $(1 - 0.1)^{10}$
   = £20 000 × 0.9^{10}
   = £6973.569

Case Study

The bank advises the Luciano family that as their lump sum would accumulate interest over time they should use compound interest rather than simple interest in their calculations for their saving plan.

**Case Study
Exercise 2**

Calculate how much they will need to invest now, at 8 per cent compound interest, to achieve £50 000 in five years' time.

Activity 1

You have been offered a new job, and you intend staying in that post for the next five years. The personnel manager has offered you two alternative salary packages; you have to choose one. All the other terms and conditions of employment are exactly the same.

Package 1: A starting salary of £16 000, with annual increments of £700.
Package 2: A starting salary of £14 000, with annual increases of 20 per cent per annum

Which should you choose?

Present value

Imagine that a relative is offering you a gift of £500, which you can either have now or in one year's time. You would probably choose to have the money now, even if you have no intention of spending it immediately. Being prudent you can always invest the £500, and in a year's time it will be worth more than £500. With current rates of interest at 6 per cent, £500 invested using simple interest, will be worth £530 next year. That is £30 more than the alternative of waiting a year for the gift. (We will ignore any inflation that may affect the spending power of your gift.)

The value of the alternative of £500 next year is worth less to you than £500 now. It has a **present value** of less than £500.

If the relative changes her mind, and offers you £470 now or £500 next year, which will you choose?

This is not quite so obvious; but you can calculate the amount you will get from investing £470 at 6 per cent per annum for one year:

$$= £470 + 470 \times 0.06$$
$$= £498.20$$

This time, the £500 in a year's time is marginally better than £470 now.

An alternative method of comparison, often used by businesses making investment decisions, is to determine the **present value** (PV) of anticipated future earnings. For example, what is £500 next year worth to me now if the interest rate stays at 6 per cent?

It is equivalent to asking: 'How much should I invest now to acquire £500 next year?'

This amount can be found using the simple interest formula:

$$500 = P(1 + i/100)$$

or

$$P = \frac{500}{1 + i/100}$$

If the interest rate is 6 per cent, then

$$P = \frac{500}{1 + 6/100}$$

$$P = \frac{500}{1.06}$$

$$P = £471.70$$

In general, the present value, P, of an amount, A, payable in one year's time, when the interest rate is i per cent will be:

$$P = \frac{A}{(1 + i/100)}$$

Similarly, we can calculate the present value, P, of a gift of £500 in five years' time, by asking: 'How much do I need to invest now, at 6 per cent pa, to obtain £500 in five years' time?' Again the calculations require the use of a calculator with an x^y function, or a spreadsheet.

$$500 = P(1 + 6/100)^5$$

$$P = \frac{500}{(1 + 6/100)^5}$$

$$P = \frac{500}{(1.06)^5}$$

$P = 500/1.338$

$P = £373.63$

The present value of £500 in five years' time, when the interest rate is 6 per cent is £373.63.

The general formula for the present value, P, of an amount A, payable in n years' time is:

$$P = \frac{A}{(1 + i/100)^n}$$

Alternatively, this can be expressed as:

$P = A(1 + i/100)^{-n}$

Remembering that a negative power means 'divide by this amount'.

Accountants and actuaries, who frequently calculate present values with different interest rates (i per cent) over different periods of time (n), often use tables of the values of $(1 + i/100)^{-n}$. These simply give the values of $(1 + i/100)^{-n}$ for a selection of different combinations of i per cent and n.

 Activity 2

An investment company is launching a new three-year investment scheme which costs £6000. In return investors will receive £1000 at the end of the first year, £2500 at the end of the second year and £4000 at the end of the third year.

If the current interest rate being offered to savers by the high street banks is 7.5 per cent, is this a worthwhile investment scheme?

Net present values

Net present value (NPV) is a popular method used by businesses to compare investment decisions. The present values of the initial costs, running costs and income streams are calculated. If a business is considering several alternative investments the net present value of each investment can be compared.

Example

Curb Ltd is considering investing in a new plant costing £68 000. The plant should last for four years, and then it will be sold for scrap for £5000.

It is estimated that the cash flows, excluding initial cost and scrap value, will be as follows:

End of year	1	2	3	4
Cash flow	£25 000	£32 000	£21 000	£10 000

Curb Ltd uses an interest rate of 10 per cent for costing projects like this.

Using the method of net present value we can calculate whether the investment in the new plant is worthwhile. Expenditure will have negative values and cash flows into the company will have positive values. The present values are shown in Table 2.1. The project has a positive net present value of £7196.37, and is therefore financially worthwhile.

Table 2.1 Present values of Curb's plant investment project

			Present value
Cost of plant	−68,000	=	−68,000
Cash flow year 1	$25,000/(1.1)$	=	22,727.27
Cash flow year 2	$32,000/(1.1)^2$	=	26,446.28
Cash flow year 3	$21,000/(1.1)^3$	=	15,777.61
Cash flow year 4	$10,000/(1.1)^4$	=	6,830.135
Scrap value year 4	$5,000(1.1)^4$	=	3,415.067
	Total NPV	=	7,196.366

It is also possible using net present values to find the maximum price, x, that Curb Ltd should pay for the new plant. This is the price that makes the NPV for the whole project equal to zero.

The calculations for the NPV of the cash flows and scrap values are shown in Table 2.2. These give a NPV of £75 196.37, which is the maximum price that Curb Ltd should pay for the plant.

Table 2.2 Net present values of Curb's cash flow

		Present value	
Cost of plant	—		—
Cash flow year 1	$25,000/(1.1)$	=	22,727.27
Cash flow year 2	$32,000/(1.1)^2$	=	26,446.28
Cash flow year 3	$21,000/(1.1)^3$	–	15,777.61
Cash flow year 4	$10,000/(1.1)^4$	=	6,830.14
Scrap value year 4	$5,000(1.1)^4$	=	3,415.07
	Total NPV	=	75,196.37

Activity 3

A manufacturing company is considering buying a new machine. The production manager has identified two possible machines from two different suppliers. Both machines have a projected life of two years, and cost £30 000. The first machine is expected to yield a cash flow of £20 000 at the end of each of the two years. The other machine is expected to yield £25 000 at the end of the first year and £15 000 at the end of the second. Using the method of net present values, which machine do you suggest the company purchase, if the interest rate is 10 per cent per annum?

Case Study

Disaster has struck the Luciano family. The freezer, which they had expected to last another five years, has broken. Carlo Luciano has spoken to the manufacturer who has offered him three possible options.

Option 1: Repair the current machine. This will cost £7500, and should ensure that the freezer lasts another five years. The freezer will not have a scrap value at the end of the five years.

Option 2: Buy a new machine now at a cost of £36 000. The new freezer should last 10 years, and will have a scrap value of £5000.
Option 3: Lease a new freezer now at an annual cost of £8000 for the next 10 years. The leasing cost is payable annually, in advance.

Carlo has produced a likely cash flow forecast for each option, shown in Table 2.3. These exclude the major costs set out above.

Table 2.3 Carlo Luciano's options – cash flows

Year	Option 1 Repair	Option 2 Buy new	Option 3 Lease new
1	£15,000	£25,000	£25,000
2	£12,500	£28,000	£26,000
3	£10,000	£28,000	£20,000
4	£8,000	£26,000	£20,000
5	£7,500	£20,000	£20,000
6		£15,000	£12,500
7		£15,000	£12,500
8		£15,000	£12,500
9		£11,000	£10,000
10		£10,000	£8,500

Using net present values, advise the Luciano family on which option to choose. Use an interest rate of 8 per cent per annum.

Index numbers

So far, in this chapter, we have ignored the effect of inflation. However, a company's prices, revenues, and profits can show a year-on-year increase, which are solely due to the company raising its prices in line with inflation. An **index number** is an economic indicator designed to show changes in living costs, or changes in prices over time.

The General Index of Retail Prices, the RPI, is probably the best known of all index numbers and is often considered to be a measure of the 'cost of living'. Many organizations link wage, salary and pension increases to the RPI.

The RPI measures monthly price changes in a selection of items – often referred to by the media as a basket of goods – bought by an 'average' family. The buying pattern of this 'average' family is based on information from the Family Expenditure Survey; a survey of approximately 7000 families keeping records of all their expenditure.

Price relative index numbers

One of the simplest forms of index number is price relative, which shows changes in the price of goods over time. To understand the basic principles of price relative index numbers imagine a family living solely on rice. As they spend all their income on rice, they are very concerned about changes in its price. Last year the price was 50p per kilogram, but this year it has increased to 60p – a 10p increase in price, meaning that unless their income rises, they will have to buy less rice this year. However, the effect of the 10p price increase on a base price of 50p is less serious on the family than a 10p increase if the base price had been 20p.

A price relative index number measures the change in price, relative to the price at a given time in the past, called the **base period**.

The price relative index number for our imaginary family, using last year as the base year:

$$= \frac{\text{Price per kg this year}}{\text{Price per kg last year}} \times 100$$

$$= \frac{60}{50} \times 100$$

$$= 120$$

Note: The price index for the base period will always be 100, since the index number would be:

$$= \frac{\text{Base year's price}}{\text{Base year's price}} \times 100$$

Many published index numbers indicate the date of the base period by printing 'the actual date of the base period' = 100.

Currently, the base year for the RPI is January 1987. In fact the actual date used is 13 January 1987. You will see '13 January 1987 = 100' as a note when the RPI is published each month.

While the example of the family who only buys rice is a helpful step towards the understanding of price relative index numbers, it is not very realistic and the shopping list needs to be extended.

If the family buys rice, meat and potatoes, all these items need to be considered in the calculation of the index number.

The prices of these goods for last year and this year are as shown in Table 2.4.

Table 2.4 Price of goods for this year and last year

	Last year	This year
Rice	50p per kg	60p per kg
Meat	£6.50 per kg	£7 per kg
Potatoes	40p per kg	45p per kg

A simple price relative index number can be calculated by totalling the prices for each year, then constructing an index number based on these totals:

Total of last year's prices = £7.40
Total of this year's prices = £8.05

$$\text{The index number} = \frac{\text{Total of this year's prices}}{\text{Total of base year's prices}} \times 100$$

If we continue using last year as the base year:

$$\text{The index number} = \frac{8.05}{7.40} \times 100$$

$$= 108.8$$

The main disadvantage of this index number is that it takes no account of the relative quantities of the goods purchased. A small increase in price of a product, which is frequently bought and used, will have more effect on the family than a large increase in the price of a product, which is bought only occasionally. Therefore, the quantities purchased need to be taken into account when constructing the index number. The index number should reflect the cost of the whole shopping basket. This is called weighting.

Again, this leads to a problem – the family probably does not buy the same quantity of each item each year. Do we use the quantities bought in the base year (base weighting), or in the current year (current weighting)? Both methods have their supporters.

Base weighting

This method weights the prices by the quantities bought in the base year. This is equivalent to asking: 'What did the base year quantities of goods cost then, and what do they cost now?'

The resulting index number is often called the Laspeyres price index, named after its inventor.

Laspeyres price index =

$$\frac{\text{Total cost of base year quantities at current prices}}{\text{Total cost of base year quantities at base year prices}} \times 100$$

Returning to our fictitious family, the prices and quantities of goods bought last year and the prices paid this year are set out in Table 2.5.

Total cost of base year quantities at base year prices
= £(0.5 × 200 + 6.5 × 50 + 0.4 × 100)
= £(100 + 325 + 40)
= £465

Total cost of base year quantities at current year prices
= £(0.6 × 200 + 7 × 50 + 0.45 × 100)
= £(120 + 350 + 45)

Table 2.5 Food bought last year, with last year's and this year's prices

| | | Last year | | This year |
	Quantity	Price		Price
Rice	200 kg	50p per kg		60p per kg
Meat	50 kg	£6.50 per kg		£7 per kg
Potatoes	100 kg	40p per kg		45p per kg

= £515

Giving a Laspeyres price index of:

$$\frac{515}{465} \times 100 = 110.8$$

The formula for Laspeyres price index can be expressed as:

$$\frac{\Sigma q_0 p_n}{\Sigma q_0 p_0} \times 100$$

where:
q_0 = base year quantities
p_0 = base year prices
p_n = current year prices.

These calculations are easily carried out on a spreadsheet by putting the data into a table with extra columns for $q_0 p_0$ and $q_0 p_n$, and are shown in Table 2.6.

(Note: you should try and use the spreadsheet's copy function when carrying out repeated operations.)

Table 2.6 Calculations for Laspeyres price index

		Last year		This year	
	Quantity q_0	Price (£) p_0	$p_0 q_0$	Price (£) p_n	$q_0 p_n$
Rice	200	0.5	100	0.6	120
Meat	50	6.5	325	7	350
Potatoes	100	0.4	40	0.45	45
		Total =	465	Total =	515

Laspeyres price index = 110.75269

Activity 4

A building company buys bricks, sand and cement. The quantities bought in 1998 are shown in Table 2.7, along with the prices for 1998 and 1999. Using 1998 as the base year calculate the Laspeyres price index.

Table 2.7 Quantities and prices of bricks, sand and cement bought in 1998 and 1999

Item	Quantity	1998 Price	1999 Price
Bricks	700 tons	£4 per ton	£4.20 per ton
Sand	35 cubic metres	£12 per cubic metre	£20 per cubic metre
Cement	600 bags	£14 per bag	£12 per bag

- The main disadvantage of a base weighted index number is that the weights (i.e. the quantities) are out of date, as they relate to the base year – not the current year.
- The major advantage is that, if we are calculating a series of index numbers over a period of time $\Sigma q_0 p_0$ remains constant, and the resulting index numbers can be compared directly.

Current weighting

Current weighting uses the quantities bought in the current year, and costs these quantities at base year and current year prices.

This is equivalent to asking: 'What do the current year quantities of goods cost now, and what would they have cost in the base year?'

The resulting index number is often called the Paasche price index, again named after its inventor.

The Paasche price index =

$$\frac{\text{Total cost of current year quantities at current prices}}{\text{Total cost of current year quantities at base year prices}} \times 100$$

Using q_n to represent the current quantities, the formula for the Paasche price index becomes:

$$\frac{\Sigma q_n p_n}{\Sigma q_n p_0} \times 100$$

If the quantities of goods bought by our fictitious family this year are:

250 kg of rice
75 kg of meat
125 kg of potatoes

then Table 2.8 shows the data required to find the Paasche price index.

Table 2.8 Current quantities of food bought

	Last year Price	This year Quantity	This year Price
Rice	50p per kg	250 kg	60p per kg
Meat	£6.50 per kg	75 kg	£7 per kg
Potatoes	40p per kg	125 kg	45p per kg

This year the costs of buying the three items of food
= £(250 × 0.6 + 75 × 7 + 125 × 0.45)
= £(150 + 525 + 56.25)

= £731.25

The cost of buying the same quantities of food last year
= £(250 × 0.5 + 75 × 6.5 + 125 × 0.4)
= £(125 + 487.5 + 50)
= £662.50

Putting these values into the formula for the Paasche price index gives

(731.25/662.5) × 100
= 110.38

Again the calculations lend themselves to a spreadsheet, and the table of calculations is shown in Table 2.9.

Table 2.9 Calculations to find Paasche price index

	This year Quantity	Last year Price (£ per unit)	$q_n p_o$	This year Price (£ per unit)	$q_n p_n$
Rice	250	0.5	125	0.6	150
Meat	75	6.5	487.5	7	525
Potatoes	125	0.4	50	0.45	56.25
		Total =	662.5	Total =	731.25

Paasche price index = 110.38

Activity 5

In 1999 the building company in Activity 4 bought 780 tons of bricks, 31 cubic metres of sand and 750 bags of cement. The 1998 and 1999 prices of the goods remain unchanged. Using 1998 as the base year calculate the Paasche price index.

- The advantage of a current weighted price index is that the weights used are the most recent, and so the index is up to date.
- The disadvantage is that $\Sigma q_n p_0$ changes from year to year, so that direct comparisons across a series of current weighted index numbers is not possible.

'Removing' the effects of inflation

One of the most important uses of index numbers is to 'remove' the effect of inflation from a set of financial information. As mentioned earlier, a company's prices, revenues, and profits can show a year-on-year increase, solely due to the company raising its prices in line with inflation. By deflating the data we can see whether or not this is the case.

In June 1997, when the RPI was 157.57, a company paid its production staff £250 per week. A year later, when the RPI was 163.40, the company increased this to £260. By taking the effects of inflation, as measured by the RPI, into account we can tell whether the production staff are any better off.

The RPI tells us that goods and services, which cost £157.57 in June 1997, cost £163.40 a year later. In other words, goods and services, which cost £1 in June 1998, would have cost £(157.57/163.40) = 96.4 p in June 1997.

Or a salary of £260 in June 1998, would have been worth £(0.964 × 260) = £250.72 in June 1997. The production staff are slightly better off as a result of the increase.

Case Study

Each year Maria Luciano makes a presentation to the family aiming to show the financial health of the business. Her presentation always includes the pre-tax profits for the last five years. The family is pleased to see these profits increasing over time. However, Maria has failed to mention that some of this increase may be due to inflation. The pre-tax profits and the RPIs for the years 1994 to 1998 are shown in Table 2.10.

Table 2.10 Luciano's pre-tax profits and the annual average RPI

(13 Jan1987 = 100)	1994	1995	1996	1997	1998
Pre-tax profit	£112,000	£128,000	£129,000	£130,000	£147,000
Annual average RPI	144.1	149.1	152.7	157.5	163.5 (estimate)

Case Study Exercise 4

 Using the RPIs, deflate the pre-tax profits. Draw graphs, which Maria could use in her presentation, to show the pre-tax profits before and after accounting for inflation.

Summary

This chapter was designed to give you a small insight into the field of financial decision making. It is a vast area where businesses need, and take, sound advice from financial experts. It was not designed to transform you into a financial expert, rather to help you to communicate with them.

You should now be able to calculate **simple and compound interest**, and be able to **depreciate** the value of goods by a **fixed amount** and by a **fixed percentage**. These skills are applicable in many business situations. For example, machines depreciate in value from one year to the next, salaries can increase by annual instalments, money is invested and earns interest, loans are repaid etc.

Net present values is one of a range of methods used by businesses to make investment decisions based on sound financial footings.

Finally we looked at **index numbers**, an economic indicator designed to show changes in living costs, or changes in prices over time. The **General Index of Retail Prices** is probably the most well-known index number in the UK and many annual salary increases are linked to this statistic.

Further reading

Wisniewski, M. (1994). 'Financial decision making' in *Quantitative Methods for Decision Makers*, Pitman Publishing.
'Index numbers' in *First Year Study Guides – Quantitative Methods*, BPP Publishing (1993).

Self Assessment 1

1. Multiple choice
Circle the response that you consider to be correct.
1.1 Simple interest is an example of
   (a) an arithmetic progression
   (b) a geometric progression
   (c) neither of these
1.2 Compound interest is an example of
   (a) an arithmetic progression
   (b) a geometric progression
   (c) neither of these
1.3 The present value of a sum of money is
   (a) an arithmetic progression
   (b) a geometric progression
   (c) the amount to be invested now to acquire that amount in the future
   (d) the value of a future investment
1.4 An index number is always greater than 100
   (a) True
   (b) False
1.5 The RPI and the Family Expenditure Survey are the same
   (a) True
   (b) False
1.6 Laspeyres price index is a base weighted index
   (a) True
   (b) False
1.7 Paasche price index is a base weighted index
   (a) True
   (b) False

2. Progressions
2.1 £200 is invested at 9 per cent compound interest, what will it be worth after five years?
2.2 How much should be invested today to accumulate to £400 in

three years' time, at 8 per cent compound interest?

2.3 How much is the annual depreciation if a machine is bought for £350 new, and will be written off completely in ten years' time?

2.4 What is the present value of £700, to be paid in three years' time, if the interest rate is 6 per cent?

3. Index numbers

3.1 What is the price relative index number of a commodity costing 15p last year and 20p this year? Use last year as the base year.

3.2 Find

(a) the Laspeyres price index

(b) the Paasche price index

for the purchases shown in Table 2.11, using last year as the base year.

Table 2.11 Self-assessment question 3.2

	Price paid last year	Quantity bought last year	Price paid this year	Quantity bought this year
Bread	50p per loaf	52 loaves	55p per loaf	45 loaves
Milk	27p per carton	200 cartons	32p per carton	180 cartons
Cheese	£3 per pack	5 packs	£3.10 per pack	4 packs

4. Exercises

4.1 InstaPrint buys a new copier for £10 350, it is expected to last for ten years, when its scrap value will be £1550. Their accountant suggests the value be depreciated by a fixed amount each year, how much should this be?

4.2 A car hire company writes off 12 per cent of the value of the cars as depreciation each year. If the company buys a new car for £15 000, what will it be worth in two years' time?

4.3 An investor has £10 000 to invest in one of two alternative investments. Investment A is expected to yield £1950 per year for six years, while Investment B will yield £1700 for seven years. By calculating the NPVs of these two investments, which should the investor choose, if the rate of interest is 8 per cent per annum?

4.4 A firm is considering buying a new machine, and requests manufacturers to supply quotes. Two manufacturers do so. The first can supply a machine costing £58 000, which should produce annual profits of £1500 for each of the next eight years. At the end of this time the machine will have a scrap value of £10 000. The second has a more expensive machine costing £105 000. This machine is expected to yield annual profits of £3100 for each of the next five years, then have a scrap value of £12 500. The firm decides to use the method of NPV, with an interest rate of 8 per cent per annum to compare the two quotes. On this basis, which will the firm choose?

5. Case study

Bob Cratchet has £5000 to invest for two years. He has been to two banks and a building society for advice. Each has given him a suggested investment plan.

Plan 1: The first bank suggests he invest the £5000 in their deposit account, which guarantees an interest rate of 10 per cent per annum, before tax. The interest will be paid into the account half yearly.

Plan 2: The second bank offers him a new account, which attracts an interest rate of 9 per cent per annum, before tax, payable into the account every four months.

Plan 3: The building society are currently offering 8 per cent per annum, after tax, with the interest paid into the account half yearly.

Bob is unsure, which of the three investment plans is the most suitable for his £5000. Assuming that Bob pays tax on his investments at the standard rate of 23 per cent at the end of each year, advise Bob of his best option.

Chapter 3

Collecting business information

The aims of this chapter are to investigate different methods of collecting data, to understand the differences between primary and secondary data, and to be able to decide, in a particular business situation, which is the most appropriate.

By the end of this chapter you will be able to:

Aims

- recognize qualitative and quantitative data
- explain the difference between discrete and continuous quantitative data
- explain the differences between primary and secondary data, and decide, in a particular business situation, which would be the most appropriate
- recognize the difference between a population and a sample
- explain several different methods of selecting a sample from a population
- design a simple questionnaire.

- qualitative data
- quantitative data
- discrete scales of measurement
- continuous scales of measurement
- primary data
- secondary data
- population
- sample
- questionnaires

Obtaining accurate and useful data is probably one of the most important facets of business today. Managers are inundated with information, much of which is not appropriate to their needs, or else it is in a form which is not readily understood. Good accurate data is a prerequisite to good decision making. No statistical analysis will produce useful information from flawed data. In fact, flawed data is worse than no data at all. There is often a mystique associated with quantitative data, giving it an importance that it does not warrant, if the actual data was either inaccurate or incomplete. An analogy which you may find useful to reflect upon is: do not build your castle on sand!

Most data is derived from a **sample**, selected from the **population**. The statistical term population is the complete collection of items that we are interested in. The sample is a selection of items chosen from the population. When a sales manager analyses sales figures obtained over a limited period and uses this as a model for future sales, he/she has only analysed a sample of past, present and future sales.

Tudor's Bakery has two factories in Rumania. He currently produces one basic type of bread, a plain white loaf, but demand is decreasing. Tudor thinks that as the Rumanians become more exposed to western markets, demand for plain white bread will decline further. After a visit to the UK he realizes that he must diversify to maintain and then grow his business. His problem is – how should he diversify?

- What products will be successful?
- What will be the demand?
- How much should he invest?
- How much should he produce?

At present he has no answers to these questions, but will need them before he can approach an investment bank for financial support.

Ideally he needs a business plan based on sound information. He decides to seek advice from Dominic Guyon of Guyon Marketing Information Services (GMIS). They discuss new markets, new product lines, the attitudes behind consumer purchasing decisions, what consumers like about particular products. At this stage they are only discussing **qualitative data**; once they consider the demand for each product, the size of the products and the quantities to produce, they will be discussing **quantitative data**. They will need to research both types of data during their project.

They agree that Tudor should remain a local baker and not venture into the national market just yet.

Classification of data

Qualitative data

Qualitative data is non-numeric data, concerned more with answering open-ended questions such as 'why' and 'how'. It is sometimes a way of determining the opinions and attitudes people have. For example, the reasons they buy, or like, particular products (books, CDs, clothes) or services (hairdressers, restaurants, transport).

Quantitative data

Quantitative data is numeric data, concerned with answering such questions as: 'how many?'. It can be used to describe market size, demand for products, and production output.

Descriptive classes

Here data is simply classified according to a particular characteristic that we are interested in, such as the colour of a person's eyes. We then count the number of people with blue eyes, brown eyes and green eyes. In order to be sure that there is no doubt in which category to place an individual item, the categories must be unambiguous and must not overlap. While this information may seem limited, it can be useful, telling us whether the items are evenly distributed across all categories, if not, which category has the most, and which has the least number of items.

Design a descriptive classification system for possible new products for Tudor's Bakery.

Ordered classes

Once again, the items are grouped into categories, but there is an order between the classes. For instance we can classify individual people by age group: pre-school, of compulsory school age, between compulsory school age and pre-compulsory retirement age, and of retirement age. Here the classes are unambiguous and do not overlap, and there is a definite order between the classes but all the individuals within a class are different.

Rankings

Items are ranked by an ordering system, or placed in order of preference. An item is placed first, another second etc. according to defined criteria. Occasionally items may tie for a position. The numbers: first, second, third, etc. are called **ordinal numbers**. This classification system is particularly useful when numerical measurements are difficult or impossible to obtain. It is frequently used in market research, when interviewers ask their respondents to rank particular products in order of preference.

The main disadvantage of ordinal numbers is that there is no guarantee that the difference between first and second is the same as the difference between second and third etc. This is often forgotten when data, which is ranked, is later analysed.

Case Study

Dominic Guyon suggests to Tudor that he set up a focus group of local consumers, to determine their reaction to a range of new products. (The focus group is a small sample of all consumers in the town, who form his population.)

The new products currently under consideration are:

- wholemeal brown bread
- granary loaves
- French sticks
- Italian-style ciabatta loaves
- crumpets
- muffins.

This list is an example of a descriptive classification, and is probably similar to the classification you derived in Case Study Exercise 1 earlier.

The members of the focus group sample each of the products and are asked: 'if this product were available in Tudor's bakery would you:

- definitely buy it'
- possibly buy it'
- never buy it'.

For each new product we now have a set of ordered classes:

1 Definitely buy it
2 Possibly buy it
3 Never buy it.

The members of the focus group were then asked to rank the products in order of preference. The result was:

1st   French sticks
2nd   crumpets
3rd   granary loaves
4th   wholemeal brown bread
5th   muffins
6th   Italian-style ciabatta loaves.

They said it was difficult to chose between the granary loaf and the wholemeal brown bread, so there was little difference between third place and fourth place. None of the group liked the Italian style ciabatta, so the difference between fifth and sixth place was large.

On the basis of this information Tudor decides that it is no longer worth considering selling Italian-style ciabatta in his bakery.

He now has to consider more quantitative issues such as:

● How many loaves of each type to bake each day?
● What should they weigh ?
● How much of each type of flour should he buy each week?
● How many staff should he employ?

Measurements

These are quantities, such as weights, incomes, ages, and factory production, which can all be measured and so have a definite position on a numerical scale. They are often referred to as variables as their value can vary from one item to another; they are defined still further into discrete and continuous variables.

Discrete variables

These variables can only take certain definite values, usually whole number values (integers).

Examples of discrete variables are dress sizes, shoe sizes, number of cars produced each day, number of items sold. European shoe sizes take integer discrete values: 39, 40, 41, 42, etc. whereas UK shoe sizes: 5, 5½, 6, 6½, 7, 7½, etc. take non-integer discrete values.

Continuous variables

Continuous variables can take any value from the scale; the only limitation is the accuracy of measurement. Heights and weights fall into this category, the accuracy of measurement depends on the ruler or scales used.

Wages and salaries are often considered to be continuous variables, even though the actual amount paid is a discrete value. The pence are considered proportionally too small to warrant treating the variable as discrete.

Case Study Exercise 2

Which of the variables that Tudor is considering are discrete and which are continuous?

Collecting data

We shall now consider different ways of collecting data. As mentioned earlier, we cannot produce meaningful information for business decision making without accurate, reliable and complete data.

Case Study Exercise 3

If you were advising Tudor's Bakery, what data would you suggest he now needs to collect to assist him in preparing his presentation to the investment bank?

Data can be collected in a variety of ways, and from a number of sources. All have different cost and accuracy implications. There are two main categories of data: **primary data** and **secondary data**. Primary data is data collected specifically for a particular project, to answer particular questions, or solve particular problems. Secondary data has been collected for another purpose. It includes data published by the Government Statistical Service, trade associations, newspapers, and even data collected by friends and colleagues.

Secondary data

Secondary data can provide a good overview of a topic, although it may not answer all the questions being asked. It may need to be supplemented with primary data from a survey. Of course, secondary data may have been collected a while ago. This is often the case with government statistics. Although the government has the advantage that it imposes a statutory duty on organizations to provide certain information – an advantage that we cannot compete with – you may find the statistics rather outdated.

Increasingly a wealth of data is available electronically, either through the Internet or via business databases such as DATAS-

TREAM and FAME. DATASTREAM is often used as a source of data by newspapers and journals for their business articles.

There are several good reasons for using secondary data, it can provide:

- general economic background
- changes in the environment
- market sizes and trends
- market structures
- profiles of current and potential customers
- market intelligence and competitor profiles
- product and pricing information.

Case Study Exercise 4

Using only secondary data write a report on the UK bakery industry that could be used by Dominic Guyon as a guide to trends, which may be mirrored in the future, by the Romanian bakery industry.

Primary data

Once you decide that the secondary data is not sufficient, or appropriate to your particular needs, the time has come to collect primary data. There are a number of ways of collecting primary data, each suitable for a different purpose, and each with its own advantages and disadvantages.

First of all, it is important to define the exact purpose for which the data is needed. This will affect both the type of data and the data collection method to be used. For every survey it is worthwhile asking what decision will be made on completion of the research to solve the problem? And how will this piece of information contribute to that?

Activity 1

Mr Williams is the owner/manager of a sport and fitness centre, currently offering squash courts, a fully equipped fitness centre, and a large hall used for aerobics and five-a-side football. He is considering a number of options to increase the business. He has the finance to extend the facilities, but is not sure which will be the most successful. He is considering adding saunas and Jacuzzis to the fitness centre, and perhaps a new 'healthy eating' salad bar. He could also replace the pleasant gardens with a free car park for customer use.

The centre is on a busy road with parking restrictions. The local council's swimming pool and library is half a mile down the road with an adjoining 'pay and display' car park. The local first division football club is seeking planning permission for a new, large stadium and leisure complex on the outskirts of the town. This leisure complex will offer a golf driving range, swimming pool, squash and badminton courts, a fully fitted gym, a licensed bar and restaurant as well as a free car park. Mr Williams realizes that some of his existing customers could be attracted to this new leisure complex.

1 What do you consider to be the problem(s) facing Mr Williams?
2 What information does Mr Williams need to collect?

Populations and samples

Once you have identified the need to collect your own data you may encounter the problem of who to survey.

This actually involves defining precisely the population (sometimes called the universe) that we are interested in. In Activity 1 Mr Williams is interested in obtaining the views of his existing customers, and so the population here will be all his existing customers. But, does this mean:

● Regular customers?
● Those who only rarely use the centre?
● Those who have only visited once?

It is even more difficult to define the population of potential customers.

Once the population is defined it is not possible to survey every member of the population. Even if it were it would cost too much and take too long.

So far we have only considered people, but a population does not have to consist of people, it can be products, volcanoes, earthquakes, bacteria etc. as the word population is used in its statistical sense.

If we were interested in finding out how long a light bulb lasts, our population would be all light bulbs. However, our survey to determine how long they last would actually destroy the bulbs in the process!

In most cases surveys are based on samples selected from the population. The process of sampling involves a good deal of preparatory work. If the sample is properly chosen, the sample results will closely reflect the population results. 'Properly chosen' means that the sample should **represent** its population, and it should be **unbiased.** We cannot just arbitrarily select the sample, or rely on volunteers, or friends.

There are several methods of selecting samples from populations, each has its own particular set of advantages and disadvantages. Several of the methods require us to have a list of all the items in the population called a **sampling frame**, before it is possible to select the sample.

Simple random sampling

In a simple random sample, every item in the population has the same chance of being selected. It is equivalent to writing the names of every individual in the population (the sampling frame) on pieces of paper, putting them in a hat, shaking well, and drawing out the required number, one at a time, for the sample. Once a name has been selected there are two options; to put it back into the hat (sampling with replacement) when it can be selected again, or to leave it out (sampling without replacement).

The process of selecting a simple random sample reflects these steps.

Firstly, each member of the population is given its own unique identification number (the sampling frame).

Random numbers, often computer generated, replace the process of putting the numbers into a hat and drawing them out one by one. The sample is formed of those members of the population whose identification number corresponds to the random numbers generated.

To obtain a set of random numbers using Excel; select Random number generator from Data analysis on the Tools menu. A dialog box appears on the screen that requires the following information:

1 Number of variables – enter the number of columns of numbers required.
2 Number of random numbers – enter the number of random numbers required.

3 Distribution – select uniform for simple random numbers between 0 and 1.
4 Output range – enter the location of the top left-hand cell of the output table.
5 The random numbers generated will be between 0 and 1. To get numbers of the correct order of magnitude multiply the whole set by 10, 100 or 1000 etc.

Example

A factory has a workforce of 7000 employees. The personnel officer wishes to survey a sample of 50 employees. The personnel officer runs off a print out of the names of each employee. These are printed alphabetically. She then assigns a unique sequential number to each, starting with 0001, to form the sampling frame.

She uses the random number generator from Excel to select 50 numbers. The numbers generated are shown in Table 3.1. As these numbers are all between 0 and 1 the personnel officer multiplies each by 7000, as there are 7000 employees in her population. Rounding these 50 numbers to the nearest whole number gives her the numbers of the 50 employees who form her sample. This is shown in Table 3.2. She then refers back to her sampling frame to find the names of the employees who were assigned these numbers.

Table 3.1 50 random numbers generated by the random number generator

0.382	0.100681	0.596484	0.899106	0.88461
0.958464	0.014496	0.407422	0.863247	0.138585
0.245033	0.045473	0.03238	0.164129	0.219611
0.01709	0.285043	0.343089	0.553636	0.357372
0.371838	0.355602	0.910306	0.466018	0.42616
0.303903	0.975707	0.806665	0.991241	0.256264
0.951689	0.053438	0.705039	0.816523	0.972503
0.466323	0.300211	0.750206	0.351482	0.775658
0.074343	0.198431	0.064058	0.358348	0.487045
0.511216	0.373455	0.9859·	0.040712	0.23072

One of her colleagues suggests a quicker method of selecting the sample. As she needs 50 out of 7000 employees he suggest that she:

- calculates the **sampling fraction**, that is the size of the population divided by the size of the sample (7000/50 = 140)
- randomly selects a number between 1 and 140 as her starting point
- then selects every 140th employee from the sampling frame

Table 3.2 The 50 employees selected for the sample

2674	705	4175	6294	6192
6709	101	2852	6043	970
1715	318	227	1149	1537
120	1995	2402	3875	2502
2603	2489	6372	3262	2983
2127	6830	5647	6939	1794
6662	374	4935	5716	6808
3264	2101	5251	2460	5430
520	1389	448	2508	3409
3579	2614	6901	285	1615

This is, in fact, a method of sampling called **systematic sampling**, where every k^{th} member of a sampling frame is selected to be in the sample.

Strictly, systematic sampling is not equivalent to simple random sampling, unless the sampling frame is in a random order. The alphabetic list of employees may or may not be a random list.

Stratified sampling

It is possible that the sample of 50 employees selected by simple random sampling did not include any women, even though women comprise a third of the workforce at the factory. Using **stratified sampling** can eliminate the chance of this occurring.

Stratified sampling is a sampling procedure used when the population of interest is divided into subgroups, all of which are different from each other.

In our example we could have just two subgroups: men and

women. Or we could have more by stratifying the employees by occupations.

Stratification means that, before any selection takes place, the population is divided into a number of **strata**, and then a random sample is selected from each stratum. If the same sampling fraction is applied to each stratum in the population (e.g. gender, age group, location) then each of the different strata will be correctly represented in the sample.

Example

To ensure that the sample of employees becomes more representative of the population of the 7000 employees, the personnel officer decides to use a stratified sample. She divides the workforce into six strata:

1 Male skilled: 3500 employees
2 Female skilled: 2300 employees
3 Male unskilled: 300 employees
4 Female unskilled: 250 employees
5 Male professional/managerial: 550 employees
6 Female professional/managerial: 100 employees.

Each stratum has its own sampling frame, and she will need to select a random sample from each. As she still wants a sample of 50 employees the sampling fraction remains at 140, but this time she applies it to each stratum, giving the following sample to be selected from each stratum:

1 Male skilled: 25 employees
2 Female skilled: 16 employees
3 Male unskilled: 2 employees
4 Female unskilled: 2 employees
5 Male professional/managerial: 4 employees
6 Female professional/managerial: 1 employee.

(You will have realized that these numbers have been rounded to the nearest whole number.)

Cluster sampling

In cluster sampling, as in stratified sampling, the population is divided into subgroups. However, in the case of cluster sampling, the subgroups are referred to as clusters, and are random groupings of the variable of interest. The sampling unit is the cluster, and the sampling frame is a list of all the clusters. For cluster sampling to be effective the clusters should have the following characteristics:

- The variation within the clusters should be as large as possible.
- The variation between the clusters should be as small as possible.

These are the opposite requirements to those needed for stratified sampling.

Example

Brutus Pet Foods manufacture a popular brand of dry dog food, which is sold in 10 kg bags. The bags are filled automatically by machine, and then packed in boxes, four bags to a box. The boxes are sealed and then transferred to the warehouse ready to be dispatched to the retailers.

On one particular day the production manager suspects that the automatic filling machine has a fault and the bags are not being filled correctly. He decides to stop the process and check the machine by accurately weighing a sample of 100 bags. Unfortunately 1000 bags have already been filled, packed in boxes and sent to the warehouse.

The population being investigated here is the 1000 bags produced and sitting in 250 boxes in the warehouse. In fact, the population can be considered to have been divided into 250 clusters, each cluster comprising four bags of dog food. Provided the fault in the automatic filling machine has not been gradually getting worse, we can consider the flow of the bags off the machine as being in a random order.

Using cluster sampling, the production manager needs to randomly select 25 boxes of four bags to achieve a sample of 100 bags. He will then need to unpack these boxes and accurately weigh the contents of each bag.

To form the sampling frame, he gives each of the 250 boxes a unique sequential number. He then uses the random number generator to produce 25 random numbers between 1 and 250. These boxes form his sample of 100 bags.

Quota sampling

If you have been stopped in the street by a market researcher with a clipboard and asked to respond to a series of questions, you were possibly part of a **quota** which the researcher had been required to achieve.

Quota sampling is different from the other types of sampling we have considered in that, once the general breakdown of the sample has been decided (e.g. the number of men, women, the number in each age group etc.) the actual selection of the individual sample units is left to the market researcher. The researcher is given a quota which could be: 15 males 18–21 years old in employment, 30 unemployed males aged 25–35, 42 females aged 30–40 in part-time employment etc. The researcher, aided by instructions and experience, approaches people they consider will fit the quotas, interview them if they do, otherwise, politely reject them. Reputable market research agencies carry out regular checks to ensure that their researchers are not filling in the forms themselves or not actually fulfilling their quota – particularly tempting on a cold wet day when no one seems to meet the requirements.

Quota sampling is a form of stratified sampling, but the selection of the individual items from each stratum is not random.

*Case Study
Exercise 5*

In Case Study Exercise 3 Tudor needed to collect some information so that he could make a presentation to the investment bank. He needs to collect some primary data indicating likely demand for the products.

● What type of sample should he consider?
● How should he select this sample?

Survey methods

The main methods of collecting primary data are:

1 Observation
2 Experimentation
3 Questioning.

Observation

As the name suggests, the data is collected by systematically observing a process, measuring output, or by watching what people do in certain circumstances. The information is obtained directly, rather than relying on what individuals say they do. The observer must be careful not to interfere in the process, and if observing people, not to make them aware that they are being watched.

Observation, either directly or by video, is a popular method of collecting data relating to consumer purchases.

Another method of observation is the 'mystery shopper'. Here, researchers act as customers and observe on how service staff respond to customers, their general helpfulness, and the quality of service offered.

Activity 2

The Newtown branch of Multifunction Bank is determined to win this year's annual 'Customer Care' competition. A month before the competition, Mr Ho, the manager, asks you to observe the branch and report back to him. What information relating to 'customer care' could you collect?

Experimentation

These are laboratory-type tests, food safety tests, drug efficacy tests etc. It is also possible to set up tests for consumers to determine their reaction to a new product or to find out how easy it is for them to use it.

Questioning

This involves asking questions using a questionnaire, either by face-to-face interviews or telephone interviews or by postal questionnaires.

A questionnaire is a set of questions asked in a specific order. All respondents are asked the same questions, in the same words, in the same order. Market research agencies, statisticians, psychologists and sociologists have spent a lot of time researching the design of effective questionnaires. Too often questionnaires are put together without sufficient thought about their construction. The result is dubious data leading to dubious results.

A well-designed questionnaire can make a great deal of difference to the accuracy of the data collected, and to the ease of analysing the responses. The questions must be easily understood and easy to answer.

Questions can be:

- closed – little scope for originality of response, but easy to answer
- open – allow originality of response, but can be difficult to analyse.

Most questionnaires use a mixture of both types of questions.
Here are a few simple guidelines for writing good questions:

1 Write simply and clearly
2 Ask one question at a time
3 Do not use too many options for multiple choice questions
4 Check that the questions are in the right order
5 Write an introduction and directions to the respondents
6 Thank your respondents
7 Pilot the questionnaire
8 Revise and rewrite the questions if necessary
9 Finally always assume that a number of respondents will misread or ignore your directions or leave some questions unanswered.

Activity 3

Return to Activity 1: Mr William's sport and fitness centre. Design a questionnaire to be used to determine the views of the existing users of the centre about the proposed options.

Summary

Collecting data can be an expensive, but always an important, task. **Desk research**, based on **secondary data**, can provide a good overview of a topic, despite its limitations. However, the results may not provide the whole answer and often need supplementing with **primary data** from a **survey**, or by **experimentation**, or **observation**.

Inadequate and poorly collected data can ruin a complete project, and many hours can be wasted trying to analyse it.

Further reading

Kalton, C.A. (1983). *Introduction to Survey Sampling*, Sage.
Moser, G. and Kalton, C.A. (1977). *Survey Methods in Social Investigation*, Heinemann Educational Books.
Deming (1960). *Sample Design in Business Research*, Wiley.

These last two books are rather old, but are considered to be classic texts by many in the field.

Self Assessment 1

1. Variables
Which of the following are discrete variables and which are continuous?
(a) The weights of 1 kg bags of sugar that are filled by machine
(b) The number of walnuts packed in a bag
(c) Dress sizes
(d) The number of days sick leave an employee takes per year
(e) Salaries

2. Samples
2.1 Why is it important for a sample to be properly representative of its parent population?
2.2 Is the trailer of a film (the sample) an unbiased representative sample of the film (the population)? Give reasons for your answer.
2.3 Design a sampling process for the following situations:
   (a) The HRM director of a manufacturing company wants to offer stress-management seminars to personnel who experience high levels of job-related stress. Before offering the seminars, she needs to be sure that there will be a demand for them, and proposes to survey a sample of employees in these roles. She believes that three groups are most likely to suffer job-related stress: those employees who constantly handle dangerous chemicals, the production supervisors, and the middle managers.
   (b) An administrator who needs to assess the reactions of employees to a new company health scheme that requires an increase in the employees' subscriptions.
   (c) A publican is considering banning smoking from the lounge bar of his public house. He wants to find out whether this

would be popular with current and potential customers, and the impact this ban might have on his business.

3. Data collection

3.1 Using only secondary data, for the most recent year that data is available, find out:

(a) How many people visited a cinema in the UK last year and the revenue per admission.

(b) The value of UK manufactured chemicals and chemical products.

(c) The number of people in Great Britain with a second job.

(d) The number of full car driving licence holders in Great Britain.

3.2 Design a questionnaire for the publican referred to in question 2.3c above to use for:

(a) Face-to-face interviews with his current customers.

(b) A postal survey of local residents.

4. Case study

The National Health Service is facing a potential crisis in primary healthcare unless more medical students can be encouraged to become general practitioners. Currently the NHS trains only 85 GPs for every 100 who retire, instead of the 150 needed. There is a general feeling among NHS managers that the role of the GP is not attractive enough to new doctors, the hours are long and there is no flexibility in employment and working patterns, although there is little factual information at this stage.

● Firstly, by using secondary data, establish some relevant background information.

● Design the appropriate methods for collecting primary data to establish the underlying reasons why medical students are not choosing to become general practitioners.

Chapter 4

Effective business presentations I

The aim of this chapter is to look at the most effective ways of organizing and presenting data in order to ensure that the results are clear and unambiguous.

By the end of this chapter you will be able to:

- produce tables of data
- plot simple statistical graphs and diagrams
- decide upon, and use, the most appropriate ways of presenting data for your audience
- critically interpret other people's numerical presentations.

- classification of data
- tabulation of data
- bar charts
- pie diagrams
- z charts

Most organizations have to cope with vast amounts of information. We often find that the more information we have available, the more confusing it can become. Much of this information can be raw data. It requires organizing, sorting and interpreting before it becomes useful information which can then be used as a tool to aid decision making. Many people find it easier to grasp the essential features of statistical information if it is presented clearly in a graph, chart or diagram, rather than as a turgid report, or, even worse, as sheets of computer print out full of closely printed figures.

Case Study

Mrs Rabina is the chief executive of a large manufacturing company. She is worried about the high levels of absenteeism due to sickness at the Newville site. She asks the personnel manager, Mr Pooley, to examine the levels of absenteeism recorded last year for two departments: Production and After Sales. There are seven grades of staff at Newville, these grades are given the letters A to G. Level A is the senior manager and Level G the departmental trainee.

Mr Pooley arranges for the data to be printed off his computer, by his assistant. The print out is shown in Table 4.1.

Each employee is contracted to work 210 days a year. Mr Pooley realizes that there is no point in going to the next senior managers' meeting with this print out because it is unlikely that any of the other managers will bother to read it, and anyway, he is not quite sure what the print out is showing. He has managed to find out that there were 1515 days lost through sickness during the year.

Table 4.1 Employees at Newville

Employee Ref. No	Department	Grade	Sick days	Employee Ref. No	Department	Grade	Sick days
1	Production	A	5	15	Production	C	13
2	After Sales	A	5	16	After Sales	F	0
3	After Sales	B	3	17	Production	G	0
4	Production	B	2	18	Production	G	6
5	Production	B	0	19	Production	B	20
6	After Sales	E	0	20	Production	B	12
7	After Sales	E	45	21	Production	G	17
8	After Sales	E	11	22	Production	F	17
9	After Sales	E	5	23	Production	C	15
10	After Sales	F	9	24	Production	C	17
11	After Sales	C	10	25	Production	C	20
12	After Sales	C	9	26	After Sales	D	5
13	After Sales	B	5	27	After Sales	D	12
14	After Sales	D	43	28	After Sales	F	11

(*continued*)

Table 4.1 Employees at Newville

Employee Ref. No	Department	Grade	Sick days	Employee Ref. No	Department	Grade	Sick days
29	Production	G	23	68	Production	E	3
30	After Sales	F	10	69	Production	E	12
31	After Sales	E	15	70	Production	E	15
32	Production	C	6	71	Production	G	5
33	Production	C	2	72	Production	G	3
34	Production	E	0	73	Production	G	7
35	Production	E	35	74	Production	G	10
36	After Sales	F	17	75	Production	G	5
37	After Sales	D	10	76	Production	G	5
38	After Sales	D	5	77	After Sales	E	12
39	After Sales	E	17	78	After Sales	F	12
40	After Sales	E	3	79	After Sales	F	11
41	After Sales	E	12	80	Production	F	15
42	After Sales	F	10	81	After Sales	F	12
43	Production	F	17	82	After Sales	C	8
44	After Sales	F	15	83	Production	D	65
45	After Sales	F	5	84	Production	D	0
46	After Sales	F	3	85	Production	D	23
47	After Sales	F	13	86	Production	F	5
48	After Sales	D	2	87	After Sales	F	13
49	Production	F	14	88	After Sales	F	17
50	After Sales	E	10	89	After Sales	E	10
51	After Sales	F	12	90	After Sales	C	12
52	Production	G	5	91	After Sales	F	4
53	After Sales	F	4	92	After Sales	F	15
54	Production	G	10	93	After Sales	F	2
55	Production	F	25	94	Production	E	24
56	Production	F	19	95	After Sales	F	8
57	After Sales	E	15	96	After Sales	E	3
58	After Sales	C	0	97	After Sales	F	15
59	After Sales	F	8	98	After Sales	F	14
60	After Sales	E	3	99	After Sales	F	13
61	After Sales	F	17	100	Production	E	17
62	After Sales	E	7	101	After Sales	E	15
63	After Sales	F	15	102	After Sales	E	7
64	After Sales	F	3	103	After Sales	F	11
65	After Sales	F	4	104	After Sales	D	10
66	Production	G	15	105	After Sales	D	0
67	After Sales	C	10	106	After Sales	F	10

(*continued*)

Table 4.1 Employees at Newville

Employee Ref. No	Department	Grade	Sick days	Employee Ref. No	Department	Grade	Sick days
107	After Sales	E	6	122	After Sales	E	11
108	After Sales	E	15	123	After Sales	F	4
109	Production	F	10	124	After Sales	E	17
110	Production	F	15	125	Production	E	5
111	Production	E	5	126	After Sales	D	3
112	Production	E	15	127	After Sales	F	0
113	Production	G	3	128	Production	F	20
114	After Sales	D	15	129	After Sales	E	12
115	After Sales	D	7	130	After Sales	F	9
116	After Sales	F	11	131	After Sales	D	6
117	After Sales	E	12	132	After Sales	F	0
118	Production	G	92	133	After Sales	D	9
119	After Sales	E	10	134	After Sales	F	0
120	After Sales	F	12	135	Production	F	5
121	Production	F	5				

Case Study Exercise 1

List possible questions that the other senior managers might ask about the levels of absenteeism at their next meeting.

Mr Pooley could make a very effective presentation at the next meeting, anticipating many of the likely questions, since most computer packages have very professional graphics applications which help with presentations of data. We will be using some of these throughout this chapter. As a first step he could organize the data into a more manageable form.

Tabulation

Simplification is the first objective of effective tabulation. If tables contain too much information they can be ignored or wrongly interpreted. The print out given in Table 4.1, the Newville Case Study, is actually a table, but, in this case, it is not an effective way of presenting information. Table 4.2, which came from *The Guardian* uses this method of presentation more effectively.

All tables must have a title, the rows and columns must be clearly labelled, and the source of the data identified.

Table 4.2 A good example of a table from *The Guardian*

Anecdotal indicators of recession

	Number of black cabs manufactured by London Taxis International	Number of bottles of champagne consumed per annum	Wait for a table at Le Gavroche	Cost of an E-type Jaguar	
1989	70/wk	24m	—	£100,000	'A glut of empty cabs touring the streets means that business is bad'
1991	32/wk	14.5m	3 months	£20,000	
1998	80/wk	23m	2 weeks	£55,000	

Copyright: The Guardian

Case Study

If we return to Mr Pooley and his forthcoming presentation, he could be asked 'Do the two departments have similar levels of absenteeism?'

Until we separate them we cannot tell. The computer print out has simply given the figures for both departments mixed together.

Totalling each department separately shows that 811 days were lost in After Sales and 704 in Production during the year, as shown in Table 4.3.

A further refinement is to classify each department by grade of staff, and produce a table showing the number of days lost by department and by grade, as shown in Table 4.4.

Table 4.3 Days lost through sickness by department

Department	Days lost
After Sales	811
Production	704
Total	1515

Source: Personnel records

Table 4.4 Number of days lost through sickness by grade and department

	Department		
Grade	After Sales	Production	Total
A	5	5	10
B	8	34	42
C	49	73	122
D	127	88	215
E	273	131	404
F	349	167	516
G	0	206	206
Total =	811	704	1515

Source: Personnel records

Mr Pooley is really feeling that he is getting on top of this now until his assistant reminds him that there are different numbers of staff in each department, and at each grade, which makes the comparisons rather meaningless!

She suggests that he produce a table showing, for each department, the percentage of the total working days that are lost by grade. Each employee is required to work 210 days a year so Mr Pooley calculates the maximum number of working days available for each grade. He then works out the percentage days lost by grade using his spreadsheet. The spreadsheet calculations are shown in Table 4.5.

Mr Pooley decides, for the purposes of his presentation, to produce just one table, Table 4.6, showing the percentages by depart-

Table 4.5 Absenteeism by department

Staff grades	Number of staff	Total number of working days last year	Number of days taken as sick leave	% days sick leave taken
Department: Production				
A	1	210	5	2.38
B	4	840	34	4.05
C	6	1260	73	5.79
D	3	630	88	13.97
E	10	2100	131	6.24
F	12	2520	167	6.63
G	15	3150	206	6.54
Total =	51	10710	704	6.57
Department: After Sales				
A	1	210	5	2.38
B	2	420	8	1.90
C	6	1260	49	3.89
D	13	2730	127	4.65
E	24	5040	273	5.42
F	38	7980	349	4.37
G	0	0	0	0.00
Total =	84	17640	811	4.60

Source: Personnel records

Table 4.6 Percentage of days lost through sickness at each grade in each department

Grade	After Sales %	Production %
A	2.38	2.38
B	1.90	4.05
C	3.89	5.79
D	4.65	13.97
E	5.42	6.24
F	4.37	6.63
G	not applicable	6.54
Departmental percentage =	4.60	6.57

Source: Personnel records

ment and grade, and to present the above detailed calculations in an appendix to his written report.

This analysis does highlight an apparent problem amongst the Grade D staff in Production, and Mr Pooley hopes that he can start a discussion about this problem at the next meeting.

Activity 1

Kavita Jones has been working on a project to determine employees' attitudes to work. She has just made a presentation of her key findings to the Board.

'I surveyed a sample of 3000 of our employees, asking them their age and whether they liked their work in terms of "Yes", "Indifferent", or "No". I had 2890 responses.

Of the 2400 who answered "Yes", 366 were in the age group 56–65, and of the 99 who said "No", 16 belonged to that age group. Of the 284 employees in the under-21 age group, 196 answered "Yes", and 14 answered "No". In the 21–35 age group, 668 like their work, while 142 were indifferent, and 25 did not like their work. Of the 1352 in the age group 36–55, 138 were indifferent.

Of course I guaranteed that their responses were anonymous.'

Afterwards she felt that many of the Board did not really understand her message. She has been asked to produce a written report for their next meeting and this time she hopes to make her data clearer to the audience.

Produce a table that Kavita can use in her report which will enable her to present her results clearly.

Graphs and charts

Graphs and charts can be an effective method of communicating numerical information. They are most effective in showing general relationships and are particularly useful as part of a presentation, or in a report when the reader is not expecting to examine the data in depth. They can be used to show trends, relative sizes of different variables, or relationships between two variables. Graphs and charts show general relationships. However, they are restricted to two dimensions. Most computer packages, particularly spreadsheets, have very effective graphical outputs that are easy to use. They simply require the user to indicate the location of the data on the spreadsheet and select the type of graph or chart to be drawn. All diagrams must be properly labelled, with a title, a key, if necessary, and indicate the source of the data.

Bar charts

A bar chart is a popular method of presenting data. There are several types available, each with its own distinctive feature:

● Simple bar chart
● Multiple bar chart
● Component bar chart
● Percentage component bar chart.

Simple bar chart

This chart is most useful for showing changes in one variable. The height of the bars represents the size and so it is important that the vertical scale starts at zero. The width of the bars has no meaning, it is simply chosen according to preference, and size of the chart. It is customary to leave gaps between the bars to help clarity.

Figure 4.1 shows a simple bar chart of quarterly sales of swimsuits (in thousands) in the Eastern Region, based on the data below:

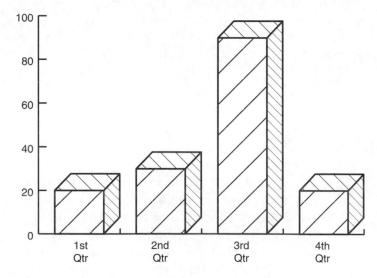

Figure 4.1 Quarterly sales of swimsuits in the Eastern Region. *Source*: Sales department records

Quarter =	1st	2nd	3rd	4th
Sales in the Eastern Region =	20.4	27.4	90	20.4

Multiple bar chart

Here extra bars are introduced to show further classification. Extra bars could be added to Figure 4.1 to show swimsuit sales in other regions.

Figure 4.2 shows quarterly sales of swimsuits in the Eastern, Western and Northern Regions. Here, extra data is available for the two other regions.

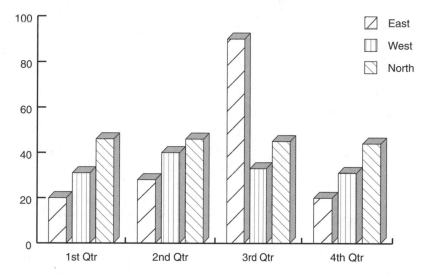

Figure 4.2 Quarterly sales of swimsuits in the Eastern, Western and Northern Regions. *Source*: Sales department records

Component bar chart

In a component bar chart the bars are subdivided to show further classifications. For instance we could show the total sales of swimsuits for each quarter, subdivided into the regions, Figure 4.3.

Percentage component bar chart

Here each bar is the same height and represents 100 per cent. Each bar is then subdivided to show the percentage of each component, as shown in Figure 4.4.

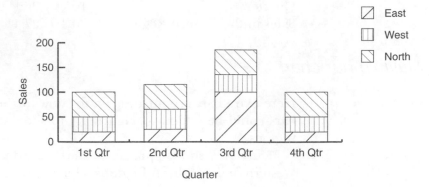

Figure 4.3 Total sales of swimsuits by quarter subdivided into regions. *Source*: Sales department records

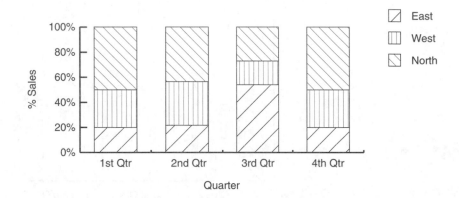

Figure 4.4 Percentage of the quarterly sales from each region. *Source*: Sales department records

Activity 2

A residents' group is concerned about the number of accidents occurring near a parade of local shops. They have been collecting data over the past three years and are due to present this at a meeting in a few weeks' time. So far they have put the data into a table, as shown in Table 4.7.

They decide that the data will be most effectively presented if they can use some suitable graphs. Produce suitable bar charts for their presentation. (You may like to try the graphics available in your spreadsheet.)

Table 4.7 Casualties by type of road user

	One	Year Two	Three
Pedestrian	17	23	37
Pedal cyclist	12	6	5
Motor cyclist	5	3	7

Source: Residents' survey

Pie charts

Pie charts are another popular method of presenting data. They are used to show how a variable is broken down into its component parts. They make a change from bar charts, adding to the variety of a presentation. They are often used in newspapers and magazines, particularly in financial reports. A typical example is shown in Figure 4.5 from BAA's Annual Report 1997/8.

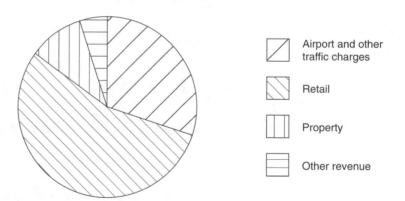

Figure 4.5 BAA's revenue by function (£ million). *Source*: BAA Annual Report 1997/8

The pie is a circle of 360 degrees, which represents the whole variable. It is then subdivided into sections, each representing a component part. Each section radiates from the centre of the pie.

To construct a pie chart we have to calculate the angle of each section, or use the preprogrammed pie chart on your computer.

Example

Returning to the quarterly sales of the swimsuits (in thousands) in the Eastern Region, which were:

Quarter =	1st	2nd	3rd	4th
Sales in the Eastern Region =	20.4	27.4	90	20.4

The total sales in the Eastern Region are 158.2 (thousand). The whole circle of 360 degrees represents 158.2 thousand swimsuits. The formula to calculate how large an angle to draw for each quarter is:

$$\frac{\text{quarterly sales}}{\text{total sales}} \times 360$$

so the angle for the first quarter is:

$$\frac{20.4}{158.2} \times 360 = 46.4 \text{ degrees}$$

for the second quarter is:

$$\frac{27.4}{158.2} \times 360 = 62.4 \text{ degrees}$$

for the third quarter is:

$$\frac{90}{158.2} \times 360 = 204.8 \text{ degrees}$$

The final, fourth quarter is the remainder of the pie.

The chart is shown in Figure 4.6.

The preprogrammed spreadsheets will draw pie charts simply by being shown the location of the data, and usually draw them much better then we can ever do.

The main disadvantages of pie charts are that:

● if there are many subdivisions the chart can get confusing.
● if you have several sets of data which you wish to compare, then the human eye finds it more difficult to compare pie charts than it does when comparing component bar charts.

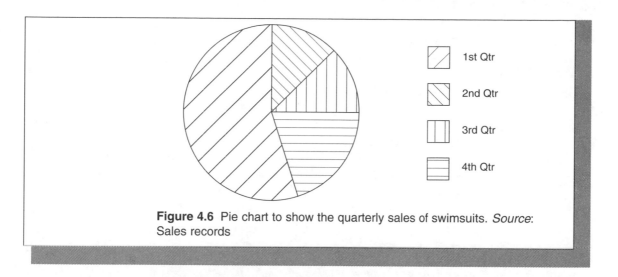

Figure 4.6 Pie chart to show the quarterly sales of swimsuits. *Source*: Sales records

Activity 3

Last year Toby Foods spent £120 000 on newspaper advertisements, £350 000 on magazine advertisements, and £1.7 million on television advertisements. Draw a pie chart to show the split of the advertising spent on newspaper, magazine and television advertisements. You might like to try producing the chart by hand and on your computer.

Z charts

Z charts are monthly records of a variable, such as sales, over one year plotted in three different ways.

- One line shows the actual monthly figures.
- Another shows the cumulative total, month by month, for the year in question. It indicates the rate of growth, or not, throughout the year.
- The third shows the moving twelve-month total up to the current month, it therefore incorporates the previous year's figures. A drop in this line shows a fall in that month's figures when compared to the previous year. A rise shows an increase on the previous year. A horizontal line shows no change.

At the end of the year, the three lines join, producing a graph which looks like the letter Z.

Example

The monthly sales of a particular brand of chocolate at a small shop for the last two years are shown in Table 4.8.

Table 4.8 Sales of chocolate

Month	Last year's sales	This year's sales	Month	Last year's sales	This year's sales
Jan	45	74	July	112	112
Feb	14	76	Aug	71	102
Mar	81	87	Sept	92	74
Apr	56	54	Oct	83	82
May	64	48	Nov	16	92
June	73	92	Dec	92	72

Source: Sales records

The Z chart will display, for this year, the

● monthly sales
● cumulative sales so far this year
● moving 12-monthly total sales.

The calculations required are shown in Table 4.9. Figure 4.7 was drawn using the Line Graph function in Excel, using this information.

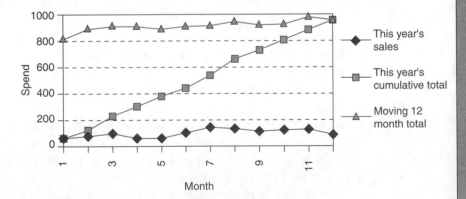

Figure 4.7 Z chart to show this year's sales of the particular brand of chocolate. *Source*: Sales records

Table 4.9 Calculations to find moving twelve-month total

Month	Last year's sales	This year's sales	This year's cumulative total	Moving 12-month total
Jan	45	74	74	799-45+74=828
Feb	14	76	74+76=150	828-14+76=890
Mar	81	87	150+87=237	890-81+87=896
Apr	56	54	237+54=291†	896-56+54=894†
May	64	48	339	878
June	73	92	431	897
July	112	112	543	897
Aug	71	102	645	928
Sept	92	74	719	910
Oct	83	82	801	909
Nov	16	92	893	985
Dec	92	72	965*	965*
Total =	799	965*		

* These figures will always be the same.
†Continue in this way until you have completed both the cumulative total column and the moving 12-month total column.

Activity 4

For the past two years the sales manager of a large retail outlet has recorded monthly sales. These are shown in Table 4.10. He has asked you to show this year's sales on a Z chart so that he can display them at the annual general meeting.

Table 4.10 Monthly sales

Month	Last year's sales	This year's sales	Month	Last year's sales	This year's sales
January	145	174	July	182	182
February	184	176	August	171	182
March	181	187	September	192	174
April	156	154	October	183	182
May	163	148	November	116	132
June	173	192	December	192	172

Words of caution

Occasionally you will find that certain authors present their data in a misleading format. Usually by false representation of the vertical scale, or even omitting this scale altogether. Try to ensure that your vertical scales start at zero; if you need to break the scale, then show the break.

Example

To show how the overall impression of a graph can mislead we can use the earlier example of chocolate sales (previous Example). Here we will present this year's cumulative sales in three different ways, just by changing the vertical scale, the data used is shown in Table 4.11.

Table 4.11 Sales of chocolate

Month	This year's sales	This year's cumulative sales	Month	This year's sales	This year's cumulative sales
Jan	74	74	July	112	543
Feb	76	150	Aug	102	645
Mar	87	237	Sept	74	719
Apr	54	291	Oct	82	801
May	48	339	Nov	92	893
June	92	431	Dec	72	965

The graph in Figure 4.8 shows the sales steadily increasing each month. In Figure 4.9 the vertical axis has been extended to show a much greater rate of growth over the year although the data is exactly the same. In Figure 4.10 the vertical axis has been compressed and the rate of growth appears correspondingly slower. Again the data is unchanged.

In all these three figures the actual vertical scale is shown, but even so the growth appears different. If the vertical scale had been omitted the graphs would certainly mislead. We can do the same with the monthly sales, Figure 4.11. In Figure 4.12 the vertical scale starts at 40 not zero. Notice how the picture has changed. There appears to be much more variation between the months. Whereas in Figure 4.13, the vertical scale has been compressed and the monthly variation seems much less.

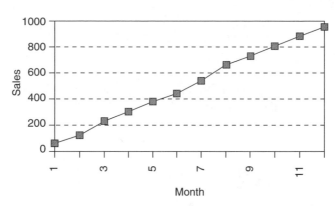

Figure 4.8 Cumulative sales of bars of chocolate. *Source*: Sales department records

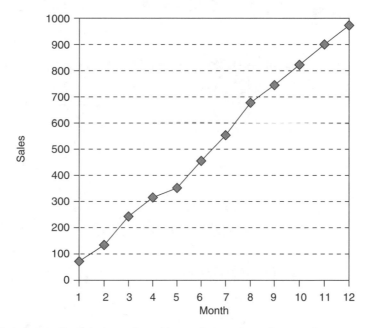

Figure 4.9 Cumulative sales of bars of chocolate. *Source*: Sales department records

Also compare these monthly sales graphs with the monthly sales line on the Z chart. These three graphs show much more variation than that on the Z chart, as the vertical scale is different.

Even the bar chart whose scale starts at zero can mislead. This is usually done by drawing the bars with different widths, or if the bars are three dimensional, with different volumes. Just to see try it for yourself.

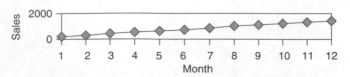

Figure 4.10 Cumulative sales of bars of chocolate. *Source*: Sales department records

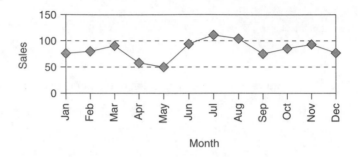

Figure 4.11 Monthly sales. *Source*: Sales department records

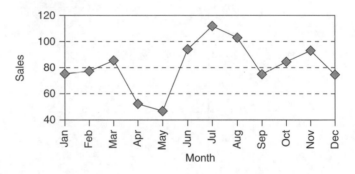

Figure 4.12 Monthly sales. *Source*: Sales department records

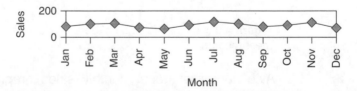

Figure 4.13 Monthly sales. *Source*: Sales department records

Using the different diagrams

There is often no right or wrong choice of diagram. This can depend on which ones look best for the particular use you have in mind. Using your spreadsheet it is possible to try out several different diagrams before selecting the most appropriate.

Before making your final decision remember that a good diagram must:

- be easy for your intended audience to understand
- show the data accurately
- not mislead.

Summary

In this chapter we have looked at presenting data in a variety of ways. The charts and diagrams, can all be produced using computer spreadsheets and they offer a pictorial way of displaying data. They are particularly useful for presentations and reports. However, we must never use these diagrams to mislead the audience and you should be aware of this possibility when we look at other people's diagrams.

Each chart and diagram has associated advantages and disadvantages. In brief these are shown in Table 4.12.

Table 4.12 Associated advantages and disadvantages of charts and diagrams

Diagram	Advantages	Disadvantages
Simple bar chart	1. Easy to understand	1. Limited to one variable
Multiple bar chart	1. Easy to understand	1. Can get confusing when the variable has many components
	2. Useful for comparing different components of a variable	2. Difficult to judge changes in the variable's overall total
Component bar chart	1. Shows the overall total	1. Not quite so easy to understand
		2. Comparisons between components can be difficult
Percentage component bar chart	1. Useful for comparisons if group sizes	1. Does not show totals
Pie chart	1. Popular	1. Really only useful for a small number of components
	2. Adds variety to a presentation	2. The human eye finds it difficult to compare more than three different pie charts

Further reading

Huff, D. (1991). *How To Lie With Statistics*, Penguin.

Self Assessment 1

💾

1. Short questions
1.1 Briefly explain the following:
   (a) A bar chart
   (b) A pie diagram
   (c) Why one needs to be cautious when interpreting graphs and
       diagrams.
1.2 What are the benefits of presenting data in a table?
1.3 Why is it sometimes better to present data diagrammatically?
1.4 When are percentages more useful in a table than the original
    figures?
1.5 What are the main items of information which should appear
    on every table or diagram?

2. Exercises
Use your computer if possible to produce the charts and diagrams,
although they can all be done by hand if necessary.
2.1 Last month the number of admissions to the wards of a large
    hospital were as shown in Table 4.13.

Table 4.13 Number of admissions to hospital wards

Ward	A1	A2	A3	B1	B2	B3
Number of males admitted	27	56	25	19	28	37
Number of females admitted	29	36	31	25	30	41

Prepare a presentation using this data for the next meeting of
the admissions team.
2.2 Table 4.14 is an extract from a set of management accounts. It
    shows the 'Budgeted' and 'Actual' expenditure on computers
    and related items for December.

Write a report, using appropriate tables, charts and diagrams
to put in December's financial management report which is to
be presented to the departmental heads.

Table 4.14 Extract from management accounts

	December Actual £'00	December Budget £'00
Computer equipment purchases	61	63
Computer equipment repairs	31	54
Computer consumables	33	45
Software purchases	210	45
Software maintenance	21	20
Software licences	20	37
Other related expenditure	29	10

3. Case study

A large manufacturing company is concerned about the apparently high leaving rate among the sales and production staff. As part of their normal procedure all staff are interviewed, by the personnel manager, when they leave. The interview records are produced in Table 4.15.

The reasons for leaving have been coded as follows:

1= retirement
2 = promotion
3 = relocation
4 = dissatisfaction with pay
5 = dissatisfaction with working conditions
6 = dissatisfaction with hours
7 = dissatisfaction with management
8 = dissatisfaction with the job content.

Write a report for the management team, using appropriate tables, charts and diagrams, based on the leavers interviews.

4. Activity

During the next two weeks collect examples of tables, statistical diagrams and graphs from newspapers and magazines. Use these to produce a report on the effectiveness of these various methods of presenting data.

Table 4.15 Leavers' survey

Grade	Total number at this grade	Age	Years service	Reason for leaving
Sales				
A	80	23	1.5	2
A		37	3	4
A		46	4.5	3
A		58	25	1
A		51	28	1
B	55	39	12	5
B		31	7	2
B		30	1.5	2
C	55	22	1.2	2
C		52	0.5	6
C		28	0.3	4
C		19	0.5	4
C		28	4.5	3
C		32	2.8	2
Production				
A	80	39	2	4
A		41	6	4
A		23	7	5
B	72	56	18	1
B		34	27	6
B		18	0.5	7
B		26	1.2	5
B		36	3.5	3
B		35	2	2
B		21	3	5
C	260	32	12	3
C		27	5	2
C		56	41	1
C		39	10	4
C		28	11	6
C		19	0.2	5
C		28	6	4
C		26	4	3
C		25	1	7
C		29	6	4
C		37	11	2
C		25	0.5	7
C		29	12	4

Chapter 5

Effective business presentations II

The aims of this chapter are to look at summarizing quantitative data into frequency tables for ease of handling and interpretation, and then to present these tables visually in histograms and ogives.
By the end of this chapter you should be able to:

- construct a frequency table from a set of data
- draw a histogram from a frequency table
- calculate the cumulative frequencies and use these to draw an ogive (cumulative frequency curve)
- interpret data which has been presented in a frequency table, histogram or ogive.

- frequency tables, ungrouped and grouped
- histograms
- cumulative frequency tables

- ogives (cumulative frequency curves)

In the previous chapter we saw that tabulating a mass of data makes it easier to handle and easier to recognize important features of the data. We saw that, if the tables were presented visually in charts or diagrams, then these features can often be made even clearer.

This chapter looks at ways of presenting data, using actual measurements such as salaries, sales, revenues, dimensions, etc. We will refer to these as **variables**. In general, the term variable is given to any characteristic which can have numerically different values. It is often denoted by the letter x. If we are considering two different variables then the letters x and y are often used.

The methods used in this chapter are not applicable to qualitative data.

Frequency tables

A large part of statistical analysis is concerned with finding out the number of times that the various different values of a variable occur, and the way that these various occurrences are spread over the range of possible values. For instance, as happens in our next case study, a café manager needs to know how many cups of coffee are being sold each day in order to help her plan her stock control.

This type of data can be displayed in a special form of table, called a **frequency table**.

Ungrouped frequency tables

This is the simplest form of frequency table; produced by listing all the possible values of the variable and counting the number of times each value appears in the data set – the frequency, often denoted by the letter f. The results are then displayed in a two-column table.

Example

The marketing department of a large chain of toy shops has conducted a survey to find the number of children per household living in the catchment area of a possible new shop. Seventy-two households were selected at random and surveyed. The number of children in each of the seventy-two households are:

2	1	0	1	2	2	3	4	3	6
3	5	1	0	2	1	4	2	2	3
1	3	1	0	5	1	2	3	2	1
2	0	3	2	4	2	3	2	4	2
0	2	1	0	1	2	2	3	4	3
6	3	5	1	0	2	1	4	2	2
3	1	3	1	0	5	1	2	3	2
1	2								

At this stage it is difficult to make much sense of the data. Certainly you can see that the number of children per household varies between 0 and 6. This is, in fact, a useful piece of information, as it tells us that our variable, which is the number of children per household, takes values between 0 and 6. Of course, we already know that the variable can only take whole number values!

However, we cannot tell at this stage if there is any pattern in the data, or if one size of family is found more frequently than another.

In order to produce the frequency table:

● list all possible values of the variable, 0 to 6, in one column
● then count the number of times each figure occurs
● and record this in the next column – the frequency column.

This is shown in Table 5.1.

Table 5.1 Frequency table showing the number of children per household

Number of children per household (the variable) x	Number of families (the frequency) f
0	8
1	16
2	22
3	14
4	6
5	4
6	2
	Total = 72

We can now see that the most popular size of family is two children, with one child and three children close second and third. Two-thirds of the households have two or more children; this could be important when considering opening a toy shop.

In a frequency table, the left-hand column shows the values of the variable. The right-hand column shows the frequency with which each individual value of the variable occurs.

It is advisable to total the frequency column to ensure that none of the data was missed from the count, or that none has been counted twice. The total of this column, $\sum f$, must always come to the number of observations, n, in the data set.

Grouped frequency tables

Often the variable can take any one of a large range of values, and each value may only occur a few times, and some not at all. In such cases, the classification is too fine and the solution is to group together several values of the variable. The groups, or classes, must not overlap and between them must cover the whole range of values of the variable. The data still needs to be scanned to get an idea of the largest and smallest values of the variable. Start the first class at, or just below the smallest value, and finish the last class at, or just above the largest value. We can make life easier for ourselves if we start and finish each class with a round number such as 2 or 10. The classes do not have to be the same size, but it can make future work easier.

Too many classes is undesirable, as many could be empty and we could end up with a grouped frequency table which is almost as big as an ungrouped table would be. On the other hand, we run the risk of losing valuable information if we make the classes too big. Grouping will always result in some information being lost and what should be achieved is a balance between simplification and detail.

Chloe Harter manages a café. She feels that her system for ordering provisions is rather haphazard, and on a few occasions she has actually run out of some items. As an experiment she decides to record the actual sales of coffee to enable her to plan her ordering. The recorded sales are shown in Table 5.2.

Table 5.2 Number of cups of coffee sold each day

56	140	71	77	68	70
83	107	59	57	84	110
78	95	58	45	103	82
99	147	72	80	55	76
56	114	71	77	64	60
102	180	104	85	91	107
97	121	106	90	121	102
58	45	94	65	87	117
64	60	67	67	94	112
92	103	63	57	91	127
135	107	65	62	67	67
94	135	85	102	68	70
85	121	84	110	49	63
86	105	97	142	84	110
75	87	94	135	89	111
73	82	91	107	64	60
74	83	59	47		

At this stage the data is not as meaningful as Chloe would like; it certainly will not help her in planning her ordering. However, if it was organized into a frequency table she may start to understand it better.

Here, the number of cups of coffee sold each day will be the variable, x. Looking at the data, x ranges from 45 to 180. This can be checked using the pre-programmed MAX and MIN functions on your spreadsheet. The frequencies will be the number of days on which each particular value of x was sold.

If we used an ungrouped frequency table we can see that the table would be rather large! For simplicity we can group the data in classes ten units wide. To cover the range and keep the numbers simple, start the first class at 41, not 45, and end it at 50, then the last class will start at 171 and end at 180. This gives us 14 classes. The frequencies are the number of cups of coffee sold in each class. This is shown in Table 5.3.

Table 5.3 Frequency table showing the number of cups of coffee sold each day

Number of cups of coffee (x)	Frequency (f)
41 to 50	4
51 to 60	12
61 to 70	16
71 to 80	11
81 to 90	15
91 to 100	12
101 to 110	15
111 to 120	4
121 to 130	4
131 to 140	4
141 to 150	2
151 to 160	0
161 to 170	0
171 to 180	1
	Total = 100

This frequency table shows the daily variation in the number of cups of coffee sold. Between 41 and 50 cups were sold on four days; between 61 and 70 cups was the most likely daily sale, closely followed by 81 to 90 cups and 101 to 110 cups. In fact on 81 per cent of days the café sold between 51 and 110 cups of coffee, and on 85 per cent of days, she sold under 110 cups of coffee. This information will enable Chloe to plan her ordering rather better than before.

A certain amount of detail though has been lost. The frequency table shows that between 41 and 50 cups were sold on four days; however, the original data contains the exact number of cups sold on those four days.

Activity 1

Table 5.4 contains the weekly wages of 84 production workers. Construct a grouped frequency table for this data.

Table 5.4 Weekly wages of 84 production workers

225	237	217	242	227	241
214	259	225	269	239	223
255	277	252	234	239	236
248	228	234	247	217	249
231	265	224	245	233	221
231	249	212	253	230	238
221	247	235	238	211	237
244	224	237	227	243	229
240	212	228	258	226	234
219	230	272	235	221	263
261	231	245	223	242	256
236	251	215	241	267	233
231	214	225	250	213	232
221	232	239	226	238	216

In Activity 1 all the wages were in pounds and there were no pence involved (the data was **discrete**). There was no ambiguity in deciding in which class to count a particular wage. However, if the first two classes were £211 to £220 and £221 to £230, where would a wage of £220.50 fit?

This is a problem that occurs with **continuous** data. In this case the class limits must be specified without any gaps.

Another problem could have occurred if the first two classes had been £210 to £220 and £220 to £230. Which class should contain £220?

Here the class limits overlap. This can be avoided by stating the class limits as:

£210 and up to but not including £220
£220 and up to but not including £230

Or, more briefly as:

£210 and under £220
£220 and under £230

Now a wage of £220 clearly belongs to the second class.

Alternatively the pre-programmed FREQUENCY function on Excel counts the number of occurrences up to, **and including the upper class limit**.

Here the first two classes would be:

up to and including £220
over £220 and up to and including £230

A wage of £220 now belongs to the first class.
Hence the need to specify the class limits carefully.

Example

A computer company operates a Help Line for customers who are having problems with their PC. Recently there have been a series of complaints to the manager that telephone calls to the Help Line are not being answered fast enough.
 The manager arranges for the response rate to be monitored. Table 5.5 gives the response rates recorded in minutes.

Table 5.5 Help Line response rate in minutes

12.42	18.64	12.36	18.54	14.66	16
11.48	17.22	16.38	24.57	5.02	7.53
13.5	20.25	19.8	19.72	6.88	10.32
26.4	19.6	18.04	17.06	10.52	15.87
19.38	29.07	11.06	16.59	10	15.48
24.66	16.99	12.42	18.63	12.32	18.54
5.02	7.53	11.46	17.22	6.38	24.57
6.88	10.32	11.32	20.25	19.82	29.7
10.58	15.87	16.4	39.6	18	27.06
10.32	15.48	9.38	9.07	11.06	16.59

The maximum time a caller waited = 39.6 minutes.
The minimum time a caller waited = 5.02 minutes.
 So we need class limits to cover the range of 5 minutes to 40 minutes. A class width of 10 minutes will only give four

classes, which is not enough. Table 5.6 gives the frequency table produced using Excel, using a class width of 5 minutes.

Table 5.6 Frequency table showing telephone response time

Response time in minutes	Frequency
5 < and ≤ 10	10
10 < and ≤ 15	16
15 < and ≤ 20	24
20 < and ≤ 25	5
25 < and ≤ 30	4
30 < and ≤ 35	0
35 < and ≤ 40	1
	Total = 60

Twenty-four of the 60 calls monitored took between 15 and 20 minutes to be answered, that is 40 per cent of all calls. The manager decided that this was clearly unacceptable and decided to employ more staff to work on the Help Line.

Unequal class sizes

The classes used so far have all been the same width, however, this may not always be the case. If, for instance, the data was mainly concentrated in a particular class, we may need further definition in this class. This can be achieved by narrower classes where there is a concentration of data. On other occasions some classes may be almost empty. If these nearly empty classes are next to each other, they can be grouped together.

Cumulative frequency tables

In Example 2 the manager was interested in response times. He might have been interested in the number of calls which were answered in 15 minutes or less. Looking at the frequency table, that was 26 calls or 17.33 per cent of all calls.

A cumulative frequency table shows the number of observations which are **LESS THAN** the upper class limit. Table 5.7 shows this for the telephone response rate.

Table 5.7 Cumulative frequency table showing the telephone response time

Response time in minutes	Cumulative frequency
10 and under	10
15 and under	26
20 and under	50
25 and under	55
30 and under	59
35 and under	59
40 and under	60 (total)

In Table 5.8 the cumulative frequencies have been converted to percentages.

Table 5.8 % cumulative frequency table showing telephone response time

Response time in minutes	% cumulative frequency
10 and under	16.67
15 and under	43.33
20 and under	83.33
25 and under	91.67
30 and under	98.33
35 and under	98.33
40 and under	100.00 (total)

Activity 2

The computer company used in Example 2 now has more staff on the Help Line. After three months the manager decides to check on the response rates now being achieved. The new response rates recorded are shown in Table 5.9.

Table 5.9 New Help Line response rates in minutes

1.2	0.72	1.63	0.97	6.93	4.15
1.35	0.81	1.17	0.70	5.17	3.10
1.83	1.01	2.91	1.74	4.83	2.89
2.38	1.42	3.47	2.08	2.56	3.04
2.37	1.42	2.17	1.30	3.36	2.31
4.38	2.62	3.64	2.18	3.21	3.25
4.16	2.50	4.38	2.62	1.17	2.22
3.16	1.89	5.01	3.00	2.94	2.84
2.2	1.32	5.03	3.01	2.28	3.74
2.2	1.32	6.38	3.82	4.21	5.05

You are required to produce:

- a frequency table
- a cumulative frequency table
- a percentage cumulative frequency table

for the new response rates. Compare the new response rates with the previous Help Line response rates.

Histograms

In Chapter 4 we looked at diagrams as a means of presenting data in a clear format which was easier than a table to understand. Histograms have the same purpose: they are diagrams which display the information contained in frequency tables. The variable is always shown on the horizontal axis, and the frequency on the vertical axis. The class intervals are marked on the horizontal axis and on each class interval, a rectangle is drawn to represent the frequency. When the data is discrete, the class intervals are taken from half a unit below the lower class limit to half a unit above the upper class limit.

This ensures that there are no gaps on the horizontal scale. This is automatically the case for continuous data.

At first glance, a histogram can look similar to a bar chart, without the gaps between the bars. There is one important difference: in a histogram the **area** of the rectangle is proportional to the frequency in that class. This will become more significant when we look at unequal class intervals.

Case Study

Refer back to Table 5.3, the frequency table for the number of cups of coffee sold at the café. Here the data is discrete and so the class limits used have to be extended to half a unit below the lower limit and to half a unit above the upper class limit.

The frequency table with the adjusted class limits is shown in Table 5.10. Figure 5.1 shows the histogram for the case study based on Chloe's café.

Table 5.10 Frequency table showing the number of cups of coffee sold each day

Number of cups of coffee (x)	Frequency (f)
$40.5 \leqslant 50.5$	4
$50.5 \leqslant 60.5$	12
$60.5 \leqslant 70.5$	16
$70.5 \leqslant 80.5$	11
$80.5 \leqslant 90.5$	15
$90.5 \leqslant 100.5$	12
$100.5 \leqslant 110.5$	15
$110.5 \leqslant 120.5$	4
$120.5 \leqslant 130.5$	4
$130.5 \leqslant 140.5$	4
$140.5 \leqslant 150.5$	2
$150.5 \leqslant 160.5$	0
$160.5 \leqslant 170.5$	0
$170.5 \leqslant 180.5$	1
Total	100

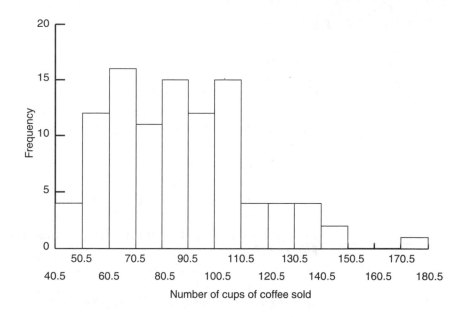

Figure 5.1 Histogram showing sales of coffee at Chloe's café

Normally at this stage you would be looking to see how Excel can help you draw the diagram. The 'Tools menu' on Excel has a data analysis tool called Histograms, which we have already used to produce a frequency table. However, the chart output is really a bar chart, not a histogram. There are gaps between the bars and, it is the height of the rectangle – not the area – which represents the frequency. The class limits are placed at the centre of the bars and not at the ends. Histograms are one type of graph which is probably better drawn by hand.

Activity 3

Draw a histogram to represent the frequency table produced in Activity 2.

Unequal classes

As mentioned earlier there are occasions when it is necessary to use classes of unequal width. This causes a slight problem when it comes to drawing the histogram where the frequency of a class is represented by the area of the rectangle. In Example 2 earlier, we produced a frequency table (Table 5.6) of response rates to a Help Line.

There was only one response rate between 30 and 40 minutes, so we could have merged these two classes into a wider one. Table 5.11 shows the effect of this. If we now draw the histogram for this frequency table with a rectangle extending from 30 to 40 of one unit high, we get the misleading impression that a large number of calls took between 30 and 40 minutes to be answered. This is shown in Figure 5.2.

Table 5.11 Frequency table showing response rates with unequal classes

Response time in minutes	Frequency
5< and ⩽ 10	10
10< and ⩽ 15	16
15< and ⩽ 20	24
20< and ⩽ 25	5
25< and ⩽ 30	4
30< and ⩽ 40	1
Total =	60

In fact, because the base of the rectangle is twice as wide as the other bases the rectangle should only be half as high.

In general:

The height of a rectangle = $\dfrac{\text{Frequency}}{\text{Class interval}}$

Figure 5.3 shows the histogram correctly drawn for the response rates.

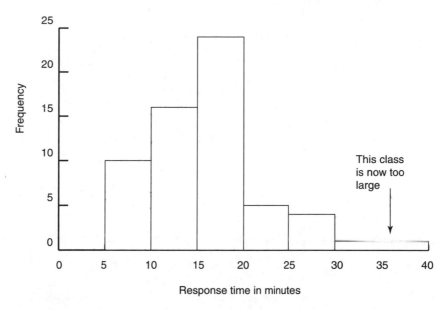

Figure 5.2 Incorrectly drawn histogram with unequal classes

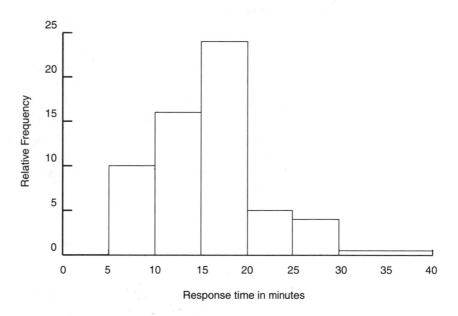

Figure 5.3 Correctly drawn histogram with unequal classes

Activity 4

Table 5.12 is a frequency table showing the weights of castings made at a foundry. Draw a histogram to represent this frequency table.

Table 5.12 Frequency table for castings

Weight (kg)	Frequency
30 and under 50	40
50 and under 60	64
60 and under 65	80
65 and under 70	72
70 and under 80	48
80 and under 100	32

Cumulative frequency curves – ogives

An **ogive** is the graphical representation of the cumulative frequency table. It is a line graph, starting at zero, which climbs upwards representing the increase in the cumulative frequency. As with histograms, the variable is measured on the horizontal axis, with the cumulative frequency on the vertical axis. The points are joined by straight lines, as it is assumed that the observations are evenly spread across each class. Steep lines between two points indicate a large number of observations between those two points; less steep lines indicate fewer observations. Ogives can be drawn using the pre-programmed line graph on the Excel chart function.

Example

Returning to an earlier example, the response rate to the Help Line. Table 5.7 is the cumulative frequency table. The ogive representing this can be drawn as a simple line graph, Figure 5.4.

Ogives are particularly useful as a tool for indicating the number of observations below a certain value. For instance the Help Line manager may wish to know the number of calls with a response rate of 12 minutes or less. This figure cannot be seen on either the frequency table or the histogram, but it can be found from the ogive:

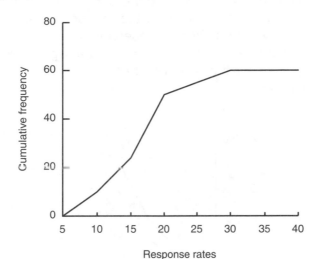

Figure 5.4 Ogive showing response rates

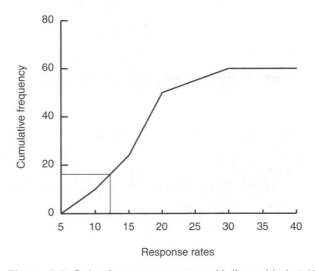

Figure 5.5 Ogive for response rates with line added at 12 minutes

- Find 12 on the horizontal axis
- go straight up from this point to the graph
- then go straight along to the vertical axis
- read off the value on the vertical axis – this is the number of calls which had a response rate of 12 minutes or less: 16.4 calls – see Figure 5.5.

If we are going to compare ogives, such as those for the Help Line before and after the new staff were employed, it is usual to draw them using the percentage cumulative frequency table. This is because the two ogives are probably based on different numbers of observations.

Table 5.8 (page 100) is the percentage cumulative frequency table for the response rates. Figure 5.6 is the corresponding ogive.

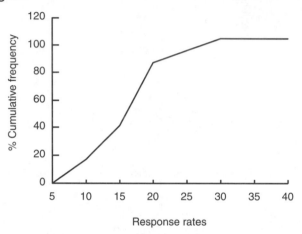

Figure 5.6 Percentage ogive for response rates

Activity 5

Draw the ogive to represent the response times to the Help Line after the new staff have been employed. How many calls have a response rate of 2.5 minutes or less?

Summary

In this chapter we looked at methods of summarizing quantitative data in tables and diagrams. We saw that **ungrouped frequency tables** show us how many times a variable takes a particular value, whereas **grouped frequency tables** show us how many times a variable falls within a particular range (class). We then looked at ways of presenting these tables in diagrams. The two we looked at were the **histogram** and the **ogive**.

Histograms are diagrammatic presentations of frequency tables.

The area of the histogram's rectangles represents the frequency in that class. This differs from a bar chart, where the height of the rectangles represents the number of observations.

Cumulative frequency tables show the number of observations below a particular value. The **ogive** is a graphical representation of the cumulative frequency table.

Further reading

Most introductory texts in the field of business quantitative methods cover this topic in detail. You might like to browse through a selection in your library, and select those you personally like.

1. Multiple choice
Circle the letter of the statement which you think corresponds to the correct answer.
1.1 A variable is
    (a) a characteristic that can have numerically different values
    (b) a characteristic that always has the same numerical value
    (c) a characteristic that never has the same numerical value.
1.2 The frequency is
    (a) another word for a variable
    (b) a qualitative characteristic
    (c) the number of times a variable occurs
    (d) the total number of observations.
1.3 A histogram is
    (a) another word for a bar chart
    (b) a graphical representation of a cumulative frequency table
    (c) another form of component bar chart
    (d) a graphical representation of a frequency table.
1.4 An ogive is
    (a) a graphical representation of a cumulative frequency table
    (b) a graphical representation of a frequency table
    (c) another type of bar chart
    (d) another name for a component bar chart.

2. Exercises
2.1 A bedding manufacturer buys springs from a local supplier. These are quality tested before use, and a series of tests produced the results shown in Table 5.13:

Table 5.13 Bedding manufacturer test results

Spring pressure	Number of springs
1.30 and under 1.35	12
1.35 and under 1.40	34
1.40 and under 1.45	77
1.45 and under 1.50	145
1.50 and under 1.55	182
1.55 and under 1.60	171
1.60 and under 1.65	80
1.65 and under 1.70	39
1.70 and under 1.75	10

(a) Draw a histogram to represent this frequency table
(b) Produce the cumulative frequency table
(c) Draw the ogive
(d) How many springs had a pressure of under 1.58?

2.2 Draw a histogram for Table 5.14, which represents the daily milk yield per cow in litres on an organic farm.

Table 5.14 Daily milk yield per cow

Milk yield	Number of cows
under 10	6
10 and under 12	10
12 and under 16	25
16 and under 20	32
20 and under 22	25
22 and under 24	28
24 and under 30	32
30 and under 34	40
34 and under 40	55
40 and under 50	12

3. Case study

A specialist vehicle manufacturer has recently received a large number of complaints from operators about rivets not fitting their sockets; some are too large and some too small. The sockets are produced in-house under a strict quality control system, but the rivets are purchased from three suppliers: A, B and C.

The specification for the diameter of the rivets is from 9.8 mm to 10.02 mm. Outside this range the rivets are unsuitable.

A sample of 120 rivets are selected, 40 from each supplier, and each measured accurately. The results are as shown in Table 5.15.

Table 5.15 Rivet case study

Supplier A	Supplier B	Supplier C	Supplier A	Supplier B	Supplier C
9.95	10.12	9.90	9.97	10.12	9.86
10.04	9.83	9.88	10.04	10.04	9.80
9.96	10.17	9.91	10.13	9.85	9.97
10.00	9.86	9.97	10.01	10.15	9.84
9.88	10.14	9.86	10.03	10.07	9.87
10.03	10.07	9.81	9.96	9.87	10.07
10.01	9.88	9.98	10.14	10.11	9.81
9.97	10.13	9.91	10.02	9.92	9.85
9.96	9.84	9.84	10.00	10.12	9.94
9.91	10.19	9.87	9.94	9.86	9.81
9.98	9.86	9.87	10.05	9.82	9.84
9.99	9.80	9.83	9.99	9.95	9.85
9.97	10.13	9.96	10.06	9.88	9.82
9.91	9.94	9.88	10.01	10.08	9.95
10.01	9.67	9.94	9.96	10.14	9.88
10.04	10.16	10.03	10.01	9.68	9.87
9.96	10.10	9.86	9.93	9.91	9.92
10.02	9.85	9.93	10.04	9.89	9.81
9.98	9.64	9.82	10.14	10.08	10.02
10.08	10.13	9.93	9.95	9.81	9.83

Produce three frequency tables and histograms, one for each supplier. From these identify the supplier(s) who are producing the unsuitable rivets.

The operators were also timed while fitting the rivets: the 40 times for fixing rivets from the unsatisfactory supplier are given in Table 5.16. Once the problem with the unsuitable rivets was corrected they were timed again: these times are given in Table 5.17. By constructing two ogives, compare and comment on the two sets of timings.

Table 5.16 First set of times in seconds

59	61	66	63	75
57	66	66	62	62
59	64	59	63	61
63	74	59	61	64
64	75	57	66	66
63	62	59	66	66
62	61	63	64	66
63	64	64	64	59

Table 5.17 Second set of times in seconds

55	52	55	52	55
53	55	53	55	53
64	61	64	61	61
52	62	52	62	62
51	55	51	55	55
47	61	47	61	59
49	55	49	55	60
48	59	48	59	
45	58	45	58	
53	58	53	58	
53	58	53	58	

Chapter 6

Business analysis

The aim of this chapter is to look at basic statistical measures. These are measures of central tendency, location and spread. It is important to have such measures; to enable comparisons to be drawn and interpretations made.

By the end of this chapter you will be able to:

- calculate the mean, median and mode for a set of data
- know which of these three measures is the most appropriate to use with a particular set of data
- calculate the quartiles and percentiles for a set of data
- calculate the range, quartile range and standard deviation for a set of data
- know which of these is the most appropriate to use with a particular set of data.

- mean
- median
- mode
- range
- lower and upper quartiles
- interquartile range
- standard deviation

Introduction

In the last chapter we looked at organizing quantitative data in order to provide an initial overview. In this chapter you will start analysing the data and calculate some fundamental statistical measures. These are measures of location and spread. Measures of location are values of the variable which are 'typical' of all the observed values of the data. In most sets of data there is some value, which may not be an actual observation, about which the data tends to be centred. Measures of spread are values that indicate how representative the measure of location is of the set of data. As it says, it measures the overall spread of the data.

Measures of location

Here we are looking for a value of the variable which is typical of all the observed values of the data. We are looking for an 'average', a single figure summarizing a set of data, which can be used for comparisons. 'Average' is a general term and there are various different types in use. We shall consider three of them:

- the median
- the mode
- the arithmetic mean.

Each summarizes the data from a different point of view and their values are usually different.

The median

The median is the 'middle' value of a set of data. If all the values of the variable are listed in ascending order, the median is the value in the middle. For example, if the weekly wages of seven shop assistants are £120, £150, £200, £120, £145, £190, £155:

- First list them in ascending order

£120, £120, £145, £150, £155, £190, £200

- Then the middle value is £150.
- This is the median.

If an eighth shop assistant had a wage of £180, then the list becomes:

£120, £120, £145, £150, £155, £180, £190, £200

Now there are two values in the middle, £150 and £155. The median is taken to be £152.5; (£150 + £155)/2, even though this value does not appear in the data set.

If we have n values listed in ascending order, the median is the value which is in position $(n + 1)/2$ from the start.

In other words when we had seven values the median was in position $(7 + 1)/2$ from the start, i.e. the fourth. When there were eight values the median was $(8 + 1)/2 = 4.5$ from the start.

Excel has the median as a pre-programmed function on the f_x icon.

Finding the median from a simple frequency table

The process of finding the median from a simple frequency table is basically the same. If there are n numbers, then the median is $(n + 1)/2$ from the start. The cumulative frequency table will help us find the median.

Example

Returning to the survey conducted for the new toy shop (see Example, Chapter 5, p. 92). To calculate the median number of children, first we need to add the cumulative frequency column to the frequency table. This is done in Table 6.1. In a frequency table the observations are already in ascending order.

Table 6.1 Frequency table showing the number of children per household, with the cumulative frequency added

Number of children per household (the variable) x	Number of families (the frequency) f	Cumulative frequency	
0	8	8	
1	16	24	
2	22	46	← the median
3	14	60	
4	6	66	
5	4	70	
6	2	72	
	Total = 72		

There are 72 observations, so the median is in position (72 + 1)/2 from the start, i.e. in position 36.5. The 25th to the 46th all have the value of 2, so the median is 2 children.

Finding the median from a grouped frequency table

Normally the median cannot be read directly off a grouped frequency table, as it usually falls in the middle of one of the classes. The values of individual observations have been lost in constructing the frequency table. The cumulative frequency will enable us to identify which class contains the median. It is then a matter of assuming that the observations are evenly spread across that class, and estimating the value of the median. In the majority of cases which involve grouped frequency tables it is convenient to think of the median as the value which splits the data into two halves. Fifty per cent of all the observations are below the median and 50 per cent above. This means that the median is in position $n/2$ from the start of the data.

Example

Return to the Help Line example in the previous chapter. Table 6.2 shows the frequency table with the added extra column showing the cumulative frequency.

Table 6.2 Frequency table showing telephone response time, with the cumulative frequency column added

Response time in minutes	Frequency	Cumulative frequency	
5< and ⩽ 10	10	10	
10< and ⩽ 15	16	26	
15< and ⩽ 20	24	50	←median class
20< and ⩽ 25	5	55	
25< and ⩽ 30	4	59	
30< and ⩽ 35	0	59	
35< and ⩽ 40	1	60	
Total =	60		

There are 60 observations and so the median is 30th from the start. It falls in the class 'over 15 and less than or equal to 20'.

The cumulative frequency tells us that at the start of this class we have already passed 26 observations. We therefore need to find the 30th–26th observation along this class, i.e. the fourth observation in this class. At this point we assume that all the 24 observations in this class are evenly spread across the class. The class is 5 minutes wide, so we spread the 24 observations evenly across the 5-minute wide class. Putting all this together: the value of the median is 15 + (30 − 26) × 5/24 = 15.83.

In general the formula for finding the median is:

lowest value of median class +
$$\frac{(n/2 - \text{cumulative frequency of class below})}{\text{number observations in median class}}$$
$$\times \text{median class interval}$$

Alternatively the median can be estimated graphically directly from the ogive by:

● Drawing a horizontal line from the median position (*n*/2) on the cumulative frequency scale to the ogive.
● From there dropping a line to the horizontal scale of the variable.
● This is the median and its value can be read from the scale.

Figure 6.1 demonstrates this. The median is approximately 15.8.

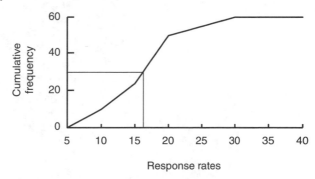

Figure 6.1 The ogive for the response rates

Activity 1

Mr Lee runs a small garage specializing in repairs to high performance cars. There are several repair bays in the garage, but Mr Lee is concerned that the garage is not making maximum use of the bays. By checking the records he can find the length of time that every car spent in the bay. He organizes the data into a frequency table, which is shown in Table 6.3.

Table 6.3 Frequency table showing the time spent by cars in the repair bay

Time spent in bay in minutes	Number of cars
up to 5	25
5 and under 10	48
10 and under 15	184
15 and under 20	196
20 and under 25	227
25 and under 30	192
30 and under 35	171
35 and under 40	105
40 and under 45	92
45 and under 50	48
50 and under 55	39
55 and under 60	20
60 and under 65	13
65 and under 70	11
70 and under 75	8
75 and under 80	7
80 and under 85	5
85 and under 90	6
over 90	3

- Find the median time a car spends in the repair bay.
- How many cars spend less than 25 minutes in the repair bay?
- Find the value of x such that 80 per cent of all cars spend less than x minutes in the repair bay.

The mode

The mode is the most frequently occurring observation. Some sets of data do not have a mode, as no observation occurs more than once. Other sets of data have more than one mode. Finding the mode takes no account of any other value in the set of data.

In the case of a grouped frequency table, the modal class is the class with the most observations. The modal class can be found from a histogram, it is the class with the largest rectangle on it.

In addition Excel has the mode as a pre-programmed function on the f_x icon.

The arithmetic mean (or simply just the mean)

This is the most familiar measure of an 'average'. Up to now, it was probably the first measure that you would have considered on being asked to find the average of a set of data.

The mean is found by adding up all the values of the variable and dividing by the number of values.

$$\text{Mean} = \frac{\text{Total of all data values}}{\text{Number of items}}$$

Or, in symbols, as a formula using the sigma notation

$$\text{Mean} = \frac{\Sigma x}{n}$$

For example, if five mail order advertisements attracted 20, 15, 11, 29 and 38 replies, then the mean number of replies is:

$$= \frac{20 + 15 + 11 + 29 + 38}{5} = \frac{113}{5}$$

$= 22.6$ replies per advertisement

The symbol $\bar{x}$ pronounced 'x bar', is used to represent a mean, calculated from sample data. The Greek letter μ, pronounced 'mu', is used to represent a population mean.

Excel has the mean as a pre-programmed function on the f_x icon.

Finding the mean from a frequency table

Once the data is organized into a frequency table, it would be helpful to use this to calculate the mean, rather then go back to using the raw data. This is fairly straightforward, particularly for data presented in a simple frequency table. We need to determine the total of all the data values, i.e. Σx, and the number of items of data, n.

In the last chapter we noticed that the total of the frequency column, Σf, equaled n, the number of observations.

In a simple frequency table the frequency column tells us how many times each value of the variable occurs in the set of data. This helps us find the total of all the data values, since

- if, there are 10 sixes in the data set, these will total 60 (as $10 \times 6 = 60$)
- if there are also 12 eights, they will total 96 (as $12 \times 8 = 96$)
- so the total of all the sixes and eights is $60 + 96 = 156$.

In general terms we are

- multiplying each value of the variable, x
- by the number of times it occurs, f
- this gives fx
- the total of all these, Σfx, is the total of all the observations
- this total is then divided by the number of observations, n or Σf, to give the mean

$$\text{Mean} = \bar{x} = \frac{\Sigma fx}{\Sigma f}$$

Example

Returning to the earlier example relating to the survey, conducted to determine the number of children per household, for the new toy shop. The frequency table was shown in Table 5.1, in the last chapter. Calculate the mean number of children per household for the marketing department.

- This involves adding an extra *fx* column to the frequency table, as shown in Table 6.4.
- This new column is then totalled to give 158

● Then just divide by the number of observations, 72

Table 6.4 Frequency table showing the number of children per household, with the *fx* column added

Number of children x	Number of families f	fx
0	8	0
1	16	16
2	22	44
3	14	42
4	6	24
5	4	20
6	2	12
Total =	72	158

Mean = 158/72 children per household = 2.19 children per household

Or

Mean = 2.2 children per household when rounded to one decimal place.

Activity 2

A supermarket is considering reducing the price of milk as a special offer to run for the next three weeks. Before doing so, the manager would like to establish some idea of the current purchasing pattern of milk. The electronic points of sale already record all purchases made by each customer, so the manager just needs to obtain a print out of the number of cartons of milk purchased by each customer. This is shown in Table 6.5.

● Find the mean number of cartons bought per customer per visit.
● If the manager reduces the price by 7p per carton, what will be the mean saving per customer per visit?

Table 6.5 The number of cartons of milk per customer

Number of cartons x	Number of customers f
0	58
1	82
2	99
3	63
4	41
5	10
6	5
Total =	358

Finding the mean from a grouped frequency table

In a grouped frequency table the values of the variable are replaced by classes. This makes it impossible to multiply the value of the variable by its frequency!

Instead we have to select a single value to represent each class, and accept some loss of accuracy. The most sensible value to select is the mid-point of each class. (This is done by adding together the two class limits and dividing by two.) This is another good reason for choosing simple class sizes. The calculations then assume that every value in a class is actually at the mid-point. Provided that the observations are evenly spread across the class, the mean will not be too far adrift. The observations below the mid-point should balance out those above.

In the previous chapter we did note that constructing a frequency table is a balancing act between accuracy and speed and ease of calculation.

Once the mid-points are known, then the mean can be found in exactly the same way as we used for a simple frequency table.

The formula for calculating the mean for a grouped frequency table is:

$$\bar{x} = \frac{\sum fx}{\sum f} \text{mid}$$

Example

Let us return to the earlier example of the Help Line. The grouped frequency table of response rates is given in Table 6.6.

Table 6.6 Frequency table showing telephone response time

Response time in minutes	Frequency
5< and ⩽ 10	10
10< and ⩽ 15	16
15< and ⩽ 20	24
20< and ⩽ 25	5
25< and ⩽ 30	4
30< and ⩽ 35	0
35< and ⩽ 40	1
Total =	60

● First calculate the mid-points of each class.

The first class is over 5 minutes, but less than or equal to 10 minutes. The mid-point of this class is (5 + 10)/2 = 15/2 =7.5

● These mid-points are then entered in a new column, as shown in Table 6.7.

Table 6.7 Frequency table showing telephone response time

Response time in minutes	Frequency (f)	Mid-point of class
5< and ⩽ 10	10	7.5
10< and ⩽ 15	16	12.5
15< and ⩽ 20	24	17.5
20< and ⩽ 25	5	22.5
25< and ⩽ 30	4	27.5
30< and ⩽ 35	0	32.5
35< and ⩽ 40	1	37.5

- The entries for the next column are found by multiplying the mid-points by their frequency, giving $fx_{mid.}$ This is shown in Table 6.8.

Table 6.8 Frequency table showing telephone response time

Response time in minutes	Frequency (f)	Mid-point of class	fx_{mid}
$5<$ and $\leqslant 10$	10	7.5	75
$10<$ and $\leqslant 15$	16	12.5	200
$15<$ and $\leqslant 20$	24	17.5	420
$20<$ and $\leqslant 25$	5	22.5	112.5
$25<$ and $\leqslant 30$	4	27.5	110
$30<$ and $\leqslant 35$	0	32.5	0
$35<$ and $\leqslant 40$	1	37.5	37.5
Total =	60		955

- The total of the $fx_{mid.}$ column is 955, this is divided by the total number of observations, 60, to give the mean.

The mean response rate = $\bar{x}$ = 955/60 = 15.92 minutes

Case Study

At WeCoverAll Paints plc the annual pay negotiations are about to take place for the production workers. The negotiations will take place between the union, which represents the majority of the production workers, and the company's personnel officer.

The company is making good progress in a competitive market, and it seems that there should not be any redundancies in the foreseeable future, but neither are there any plans to increase the workforce.

Table 6.9 shows the weekly gross earnings of a sample of production workers over one month, presented in a frequency table. Many production workers are regularly undertaking overtime and weekend working, and this is evident in the variations of earnings.

Table 6.9 Frequency table showing the weekly earnings at WeCoverAll plc

Weekly earnings (£)	Number of employees
under 100	12
100 and under 110	48
110 and under 120	119
120 and under 130	184
130 and under 140	210
140 and under 150	225
150 and under 160	193
160 and under 170	184
170 and under 180	151
180 and under 190	103
190 and under 200	99
200 and under 220	37
220 and under 240	28
240 and under 260	12
260 and under 300	5

Inflation is currently running at 2.5 per cent per annum. The personnel officer decides to offer an increase of 2.2 per cent. He considers the production workers are paid above the industry norm of £150, and rather hopes that the government prediction of a lower inflation rate next year will happen. To support his argument he calculates the average weekly wage as £153.40. The supporting calculations, for the mean weekly wage, are given in Table 6.10.

A 2.2 per cent increase on this will give a new mean weekly wage of £156.50. He is fairly confident that his offer will be accepted, but is prepared to increase it to 2.4 per cent if pushed.

He is rather taken aback at his first meeting with the union representatives who dispute his average weekly wage of £153.40. The union negotiator confidently tells him that the average weekly wage is £145, and his members are expecting an increase to bring them up to the industry norm plus an increase to cover inflation. In fact he is asking for an increase which will bring the average wage to £153.75.

Table 6.10 Calculations to find the mean earnings

Weekly earnings (£)	Number of employees	Mid-point	fx_{mid}
under 100	12	50	600
100 and under 110	48	105	5040
110 and under 120	119	115	13685
120 and under 130	184	125	23000
130 and under 140	210	135	28350
140 and under 150	225	145	32625
150 and under 160	193	155	29915
160 and under 170	184	165	30360
170 and under 180	151	175	26425
180 and under 190	103	185	19055
190 and under 200	99	195	19305
200 and under 220	37	210	7770
220 and under 240	28	230	6440
240 and under 260	12	250	3000
260 and under 300	5	280	1400
Total=	1610		246970

The personnel officer is confused, how can the average be £145 when he has calculated it to be £153.40? In fact the union negotiator has used the same set of data, but has chosen the mid-point of the modal class as his measure of the average.

Until the two sides can agree on the current average wage they cannot possibly start to negotiate the increase. If £145 is right the union is asking for an increase of 6 per cent, across the board.

After some weeks of negotiation and discussion on the current wages, the two sides decide to settle on the median as the most appropriate measure of the average. It is seen as a fairer measure. The size of the mean has been influenced by the level of weekend working and overtime undertaken by a few employees, and the mode underestimates the earnings.

The median is £150.36 per week. The calculations are shown in Table 6.11. This figure is then used as a basis for settling next year's wage increase.

Table 6.11 Calculations to find the median earnings

Weekly earnings	Cumulative frequency	
under 100	12	
under 110	60	
under 120	179	
under 130	363	
under 140	573	
under 150	798	
under 160	991	←median class
under 170	1175	
under 180	1326	
under 190	1429	
under 200	1528	
under 220	1565	
under 240	1593	
under 260	1605	
under 300	1610	

Activity 3

The turnround time of an aircraft is the time that elapses between its arrival at an airport and being ready for take off again. The turnround time for 100 aircraft has been recorded at a regional airport, and is given in Table 6.12. Use this data to calculate the mean turnround time for aircraft at this airport.

Table 6.12 Aircraft turnround times

Turnround time (minutes)	Number of aircraft
5 and under 10	4
10 and under 15	22
15 and under 20	28
20 and under 25	18
25 and under 30	12
30 and under 35	9
35 and under 40	4
40 and under 45	3
Total =	100

Measures of variation

While an average will summarize a set of data, on its own it is not usually a sufficient description of the data.

Consider the weekly commissions earned by two salespersons, Smith and Jones, over the same seven-week period:

Smith   £49, £43, £61, £47, £39, £54, £57
Jones   £31, £58, £0, £41, £101, £69, £50

Just looking at the two sets of commissions we can see that Smith's sales figures are far less variable than Jones's. Jones is just as likely to take no orders as to obtain a bumper order. Jones's weekly commission is far more variable than Smith's.

However, if we calculate the mean commission for each salesperson, we find that each has a mean of £50 per week. In this case, by just quoting the mean commissions, we lose sight of the main difference between the two sets of data.

Measurement of variation is therefore an important aspect of data analysis. It gives us a measure of the dispersion or spread of the data. It shows how closely the data is clustered around the average. If the chosen measure of variation is a relatively small number, it tells us that the data is clustered around the average; if it is a large number, then the data is widely spread out.

There are three measures of variation that we will consider:

- the range
- the quartile range
- the standard deviation.

The range

The range is the simplest measure of variation. It is the difference between the largest and smallest numbers in the data set. Returning to the salespersons' commission:

Smith's range is £61 − £39 = £22
Jones's range is £101 − £0 = £101

Using this measure, Jones's commission appears to be over four times more variable than Smith's.

The main disadvantage of the range is that it is influenced by abnormally high or low values. However, it is easily understood and requires the minimum of calculation. Because of this it is used in statistical quality control as a quick check on the variability of materials, processes or products.

Interquartile range

The main disadvantage of the range could be overcome if the extreme values of the data were not used to calculate the range, but if two values, one at each end of the central 50 per cent of the data were used instead. Then we would not be using the highest 25 per cent nor the lowest 25 per cent of the data in the calculation, as these values might not be typical.

The values used are the first or lower quartile (Q1) and the third or upper quartile (Q3), and the difference between them is called the interquartile range.

Twenty-five per cent of the data lies below the lower quartile, Q1, and 25 per cent lies above the upper quartile, Q3.

We have already met the second quartile, as this is the median. Fifty per cent of the data is below and 50 per cent is above the median.

Just as the median was the value of the $(n + 1)/2^{th}$ item in a list of ungrouped data, the lower quartile, Q1, is the value of the $(n + 1)/4^{th}$ item and the upper quartile, Q3, is the value of the $3(n + 1)/4^{th}$ item.

Excel has the quartile as pre-programmed functions on the f_x icon. The lower is specified by entering 1 into the 'quart box', and the upper by entering 3 into this box.

For grouped data the quartiles are found from either the cumulative frequency table, or the ogive. Twenty-five per cent of the data is below the lower quartile and 25 per cent of the data is above the upper quartile. The interquartile range = Q3 – Q1.

Example

Returning to the second example in this chapter, the Help Line example, find the quartiles and the interquartile range for this set of data.

Table 6.2 shows the frequency table with the cumulative frequency column added. There are 60 observations, and so the lower quartile is 15th from the start and the upper quartile is 45th from the start.

The simplest way of finding the quartiles is from the ogive. Figure 6.2 shows the ogive for the response rates with the quartiles marked.

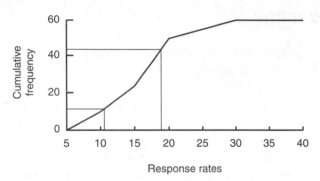

Figure 6.2 The ogive for the response rates

The lower quartile is 10.3 and the upper quartile is 19.0. The interquartile range is 19.0 − 10.3 = 8.7. This tells us that the middle 50 per cent of all responses are between 10.3 minutes and 19.0 minutes. The median response time was 15.8 minutes.

The upper quartile is nearer to the median (19.0 − 15.8 = 3.2) than the lower quartile (15.8 − 10.3 = 5.5). This indicates that the middle 50 per cent of the data is skewed.

If the data had been symmetrical around the median, then Q1 and Q3 would be the same distance from the median.

Activity 4

Return to Activity 1, Mr Lee's garage. The time spent by each car in the repair bay is shown in Table 6.3. Find:

● the upper quartile
● the lower quartile
● the interquartile range.

Standard deviation

The standard deviation is a measure of variation which is based on all the observations in a set of data rather than on just two values, which is the case for both the range and the interquartile range. The standard deviation measures the spread around the mean.

The calculation for the standard deviation is based on the distance that each observation is from the mean, called the deviation from the mean. A small value of the standard deviation indicates that the data is clustered around the mean, a large value indicates that the data is widely spread out.

If we return to the two salespersons, Smith and Jones, and their weekly commissions, as Jones's commission is more variable than Smith's we would expect Jones's standard deviation to be larger than Smith's. For reference the data is given below:

Smith £49, £43, £61, £47, £39, £54, £57
Jones £31, £58, £0, £41, £101, £69, £50

The mean weekly commission for each of the salespersons is £50 per week.

We shall develop the formula for the standard deviation using Smith's commission.

- First calculate the mean, this is £50 per week.
- Subtracting the mean from each observation $(x - \bar{x})$ gives the distance that each observation is from the mean, i.e. the deviation from the mean. Table 6.13 shows this.

Table 6.13 Smith's commission

x	$x - \bar{x}$	$(x - \bar{x})$
49	49–50	−1
43	43–50	−7
61	61–50	11
47	47–50	−3
39	39–50	−11
54	54–50	4
57	57–50	7
Total = 350		0
Mean = 50		

There are now seven deviations from the mean, and we need just one summary measure. As a first thought we could find the mean of these seven deviations as the summary measure. However, there is a snag. The sum of the deviations from the mean is zero.

It will always be zero, as the observations below the mean balance out with those above. Some of the numbers are positive and others are negative. We could try ignoring this by using the absolute value of the deviation without the sign, but this causes difficulties with further calculations. (There is a measure, called the mean deviation, which does just this.)

There is a mathematical way of effectively losing the minus signs, yet treating the positive numbers and the negative numbers in exactly the same way. That is to square all the deviations. Then we can find the mean of the squared deviations. This is done in Table 6.14.

Table 6.14   Smith's commission

x	$x - \bar{x}$	$(x - \bar{x})$	$(x - \bar{x})^2$
49	49–50	−1	1
43	43–50	−7	49
61	61–50	11	121
47	47–50	−3	9
39	39–50	−11	121
54	54–50	4	16
57	57 –50	7	49
Total = 350		0	366
Mean = 50			

The total of the squared deviations is 366 and as there were seven observations, dividing 366 by 7 gives 52.28. This number is called the **variance**. As it is based on squared numbers it is in squared units, in this case squared pounds! A more useful figure would be in the original units – in this case pounds.

The standard deviation is the square root of the variance. So, the last step in finding the standard deviation is to take the square root of the variance, thus reverting to the original units. For our data, the square root of 52.28 is 7.23.

Smith's weekly commission has a mean of £50 and a standard deviation of £7.23. Clearly £7.23 is a fairly small number when compared with £50, so we have a small standard deviation, reflecting the fact that the data was clustered around the mean.

Before we look at the formula for the standard deviation try Activity 5.

Activity 5

Use Jones's weekly commission and calculate the standard deviation for this set of data. Remember, that as the data was more widely spread than Smith's the standard deviation will be larger.

By recapping on the steps to find the standard deviation, we can develop the formula. To calculate the standard deviation:

- find the mean, $\bar{x}$
- subtract the mean from each observation, the deviations from the mean, $(x - \bar{x})$
- square these deviations, $(x - \bar{x})^2$
- total the squared deviations, $\Sigma(x - \bar{x})^2$
- divide by the number of deviations,

$$\frac{\Sigma(x - \bar{x})^2}{n}$$

- take the square root

$$\sqrt{\frac{\Sigma(x - \bar{x})^2}{n}}$$

This is the formula for the standard deviation.

$$\text{Standard deviation} = \sqrt{\frac{\Sigma(x - \bar{x})^2}{n}}$$

An alternative version of this formula derived by algebraic manipulation, which we will not worry about here, gives:

$$\text{Standard deviation} = \sqrt{\frac{\Sigma x^2}{n} - \bar{x}^2}$$

This version can be quicker when using a calculator to find the standard deviation. Particularly if you use the memory, M+, button, to add up the x^2. Only one subtraction is required, just before taking the square root.

The sample standard deviation is denoted by s, and the population standard deviation by the Greek letter σ, this is the lower case sigma, not to be confused with Σ, the upper case sigma, which means add up.

As the standard deviation is a frequently used statistic it is pre-programmed on many calculators and computer packages. Excel has the standard deviation as a pre-programmed function on the f_x icon.

Standard deviation for grouped data

In the same way that the formula for the mean changed for grouped data, so does the formula for the standard deviation. For grouped data we have to incorporate the use of frequencies into the formula.

$$\text{Standard deviation} = \sqrt{\frac{\Sigma f x^2}{\Sigma f} - \bar{x}^2}$$

Note: in $\Sigma f x^2$ only the x is squared not the f. If you prefer think of $\Sigma f x^2$ as $\Sigma f(xx)$.

Example

Returning to the earlier example relating to the survey conducted to determine the number of children per household for the new toy shop. The frequency table, with the fx column, is shown in Table 6.4. The mean number of children per household was found to be 2.2 (rounded to one decimal place). To calculate the standard deviation(s) we need another column, fx^2. This is shown in Table 6.15.

The values needed for the formula are:

- $\Sigma f = 72$
- $\Sigma f x^2 = 498$
- $\bar{x} = 2.19$ to two decimal places.

Putting these into the formula gives:

$$s = \sqrt{\frac{498}{72} - (2.19)^2}$$

$$s = \sqrt{6.917 - 4.796}$$

$$s = \sqrt{2.121}$$

s = 1.5 children (to one decimal place).

Although 1.5 seems a small number it needs to be compared with a mean of 2.2 children per household.

Table 6.15 Toy shop survey

Number of children x	Number of families f	fx	fx^2
0	8	0	0
1	16	16	16
2	22	44	88
3	14	42	126
4	6	24	96
5	4	20	100
6	2	12	72
Total =	72	158	498

Activity 6

Return to Activity 2 where a supermarket was considering reducing the price of milk as a special offer. The current purchasing pattern of milk is shown in Table 6.5. Find the standard deviation of the number of cartons of milk bought per customer.

Finding the standard deviation from a grouped frequency table

Once again this follows the same pattern as the calculation of the mean. You will remember that the data was put into classes and, for the purpose of calculation, each class was represented by its mid-point. Following this approach the formula for the standard deviation, for data presented in a grouped frequency table is:

$$\text{Standard deviation} = \sqrt{\frac{\Sigma f x_{\text{mid}}^2 - \bar{x}^2}{\Sigma f}}$$

Again in $\Sigma f x_{\text{mid}}^2$ only the x_{mid} is squared, not the f.
$\left(\Sigma f x_{\text{mid}}^2 = \Sigma f x_{\text{mid}} x_{\text{mid}}\right)$

Example

Let us return to the earlier example of the Help Line. The grouped frequency table of response rates, with the mid-points and the fx_{mid} column is given in Table 6.8. We need to add a new column for fx_{mid}^2. This is shown on Table 6.16. The mean, which was calculated earlier = 15.91667.

Table 6.16 Frequency table showing telephone response time

Response time in minutes	Frequency f	Mid-point of class x_{mid}	fx_{mid}	$fx_{mid}x_{mid}$
5< and ⩽ 10	10	7.5	75	562.5
10< and ⩽ 15	16	12.5	200	2500
15< and ⩽ 20	24	17.5	420	7350
20< and ⩽ 25	5	22.5	112.5	2531.25
25< and ⩽ 30	4	27.5	110	3025
30< and ⩽ 35	0	32.5	0	0
35< and ⩽ 40	1	37.5	37.5	1406.25
Total =	60		955	17375

Putting the values into the formula:

$$\text{Standard deviation} = \sqrt{\frac{\Sigma fx^2_{mid}}{\Sigma f} - \bar{x}^2}$$

$$\text{Standard deviation} = \sqrt{\frac{17375}{60} - (15.91667)^2}$$

$$= \sqrt{289.58 - 253.34}$$

$$= \sqrt{36.24}$$

$$= 6.02$$

Activity 7

Return to Activity 2 in the previous chapter. Here the Help Line manager had employed extra staff in order to reduce the response time for callers. Find the new mean response time and the standard deviation of the new response time. What do these figures show?

Case Study

WeCoverAll Paints plc produce two types of vinyl matt paint, one with added silk and one without. The customer services manager is receiving complaints that the paint with added silk appears to take longer to dry than the plain matt paint. She asks the R&D department to test the drying times of both paints under normal domestic conditions. These times are recorded and the results presented in Table 6.17.

The testers calculate the mean drying time for both types of paint, as shown in Table 6.18.

There is very little difference between the two. Plain matt has a mean drying time of 4.17 hours and matt with added silk has a drying time of 4.14 hours. This is certainly not enough of a difference for customers to complain. The reason must lie elsewhere.

Table 6.17 WeCoverAll Paints

| | Number of samples of: | |
Drying times (hours)	Plain matt f	Matt with added silk f
1 to under 2	14	31
2 to under 3	26	26
3 to under 4	38	23
4 to under 5	46	35
5 to under 6	22	21
6 to under 7	18	16
7 to under 8	6	18
Total	170	170

Table 6.18 Drying times (hours)

	x_{mid}	f	fx_{mid}
Plain matt			
	1.5	14	21
	2.5	26	65
	3.5	38	133
	4.5	46	207
	5.5	22	121
	6.5	18	117
	7.5	6	45
Total =		170	709
Mean =		4.170588	
With added silk			
	1.5	31	46.5
	2.5	26	65
	3.5	23	80.5
	4.5	35	157.5
	5.5	21	115.5
	6.5	16	104
	7.5	18	135
Total =		170	704
Mean =		4.141176	

Looking at the two frequency tables, the paint with added silk seems to have a more variable drying time. The testers decide to check this by calculating the standard deviations. Table 6.19 shows these calculations.

Table 6.19 Drying times (hours)

	x_{mid}	f	fx_{mid}	$fx_{mid}x_{mid}$
Plain matt				
	1.5	14	21	31.5
	2.5	26	65	162.5
	3.5	38	133	465.5
	4.5	46	207	931.5
	5.5	22	121	665.5
	6.5	18	117	760.5
	7.5	6	45	337.5
Total =		170	709	3354.5
Mean =	4.170588			
Standard deviation = 1.529231				
With added silk				
	1.5	31	46.5	69.75
	2.5	26	65	162.5
	3.5	23	80.5	281.75
	4.5	35	157.5	708.75
	5.5	21	115.5	635.25
	6.5	16	104	676
	7.5	18	135	1012.5
Total =		170	704	3546.5
Mean =	4.141176			
Standard deviation = 1.926765				

There is a difference in the two standard deviations. The plain matt paint has a standard deviation of 1.53 hours, while the paint with added silk has a standard deviation of 1.93 hours.

The customer services manager thinks about this outcome and comes to the conclusion that, while the paints do have similar mean drying times, the paint with added silk has a more variable drying time. Only the customers whose paint with added silk is taking longer to dry are complaining, not those whose paint is drying quicker. She decides to ask the R&D department if they can make the drying time of the matt with added silk less variable.

Summary

In this chapter we considered three measures of location, which we defined as a value of the variable which is typical of all the observed values of the data. We were looking for an 'average', a single figure summarizing a set of data, which could be used for comparisons. The measures we considered were the **median**, the **mode** and the **arithmetic mean**. Each measure has its own set of advantages and disadvantages. The nature of the data will usually determine which is the most appropriate measure to use.

We also discovered that these measures alone were not sufficient to summarize a set of data, and we needed a measure of 'spread'. The measures we considered were the **interquartile range** and the **standard deviation**. The interquartile range was the most appropriate measure of spread to use with the median, and the standard deviation with the mean.

Further reading

These particular topics are covered in all the basic business studies quantitative methods texts. Some give the topics a more mathematical treatment than used here.

🖫

1 Multiple choice

Circle the letter of the statement which you think corresponds to the correct answer.

1.1 In a set of data the median is:
   (a) the most frequently occurring observation
   (b) the middle observation
   (c) the weighted average.

1.2 In a set of data the mode is:
   (a) the most frequently occurring observation
   (b) the middle observation
   (c) the weighted average.

1.3 The measure of location which can be used for further mathematical process is the:
   (a) mean
   (b) median
   (c) mode.

1.4 The measure of location which can be affected by extreme values is the:

(a) mean

(b) median

(c) mode.

1.5 The measure of location which uses every value in the data set is the:

(a) mode

(b) median

(c) mean.

1.6 When a frequency distribution is symmetrical then the:

(a) mean is bigger than the median

(b) mode is bigger than the mean

(c) mean, median and mode have the same value.

1.7 The standard deviation measures the spread around:

(a) the mean

(b) the mode

(c) the median.

1.8 The interquartile range is the difference:

(a) between the largest and smallest observation

(b) between the upper quartile and the median

(c) between the median and the lower quartile

(d) between the upper and the lower quartile.

2. Explain

2.1 Why statistics calculated from raw data are more accurate than statistics calculated using the frequency table.

2.2 If this is the case why does one use the frequency table as a basis for calculating statistics?

2.3 Why, for a given set of data, is the median sometimes smaller than the mean?

3. Exercises

3.1 The mean of the following set of numbers is 5 and the mode is 4:

3   7 x 9   4   2 y

(a) What are the values of x and y?

(b) What is the median?

3.2 In 14 consecutive weeks a sales representative's commission was: £25, £17, £48, £21, £30, £44, £48, £0, £15, £20, £53, £60, £84, £13

(a) Find the mean weekly commission.

(b) If, in the next eight weeks the commission was such that the mean commission for the whole 22-week period was £3.50 less than the mean for the first 14 weeks (the value found in part a), what was the mean commission for the last eight weeks?

3.3 120 data entry clerks were timed entering a purchase order into their computers. The times to the nearest second are shown below:

number of seconds:	number of clerks:
10	2
20	3
30	5
40	10
50	15
60	30
70	25
80	15
90	10
100	5
	Total = 120

Calculate:

(a) the mean time to complete an entry

(b) the standard deviation of the time

(c) the number of clerks who took longer than the mean time plus one standard deviation.

3.4 A bedding manufacturer buys springs from a local supplier. These are quality tested before use. A series of tests produced the results shown in Table 6.20.

Table 6.20 Bedding manufacturer test results

Spring pressure	Number of springs
1.30 and under 1.35	12
1.35 and under 1.40	34
1.40 and under 1.45	77
1.45 and under 1.50	145
1.50 and under 1.55	182
1.55 and under 1.60	171
1.60 and under 1.65	80
1.65 and under 1.70	39

Using either the cumulative frequency table or the ogive that you found in the self-assessment in the last chapter, find:

(a) the median

(b) the upper and lower quartiles
(c) the interquartile range
(d) the mean
(e) the standard deviation.

4. Case studies

4.1 A small family hotel employs just one receptionist. Over the past six weeks the receptionist worked the following overtime:
19 hours, 22 hours, 23 hours, 25 hours, 27 hours, and 28 hours. Find:

(a) the mean and standard deviation of the overtime that the receptionist worked.

(b) If a part-time receptionist had been employed, who worked 19 hours each week, what would the mean and standard deviation of the remaining overtime have been?

(c) If the part-time receptionist had worked 23 hours each week, what would be the mean and standard deviation of the overtime?

(d) The receptionist is paid £160 for a 40-hour week, and overtime is paid at time and a half. The plan is to pay the part-time receptionist at the same hourly rate. Should the hotel employ the part-time receptionist for 19 hours, or for 23 hours each week?

(e) Instead of employing the part-time receptionist, the hotel could use an agency who supply temporary staff to the hotel trade. A local agency can supply a receptionist on a weekly basis, at a cost of £6 per hour for the first five hours. The next five are charged at time and a quarter, and the remainder are charged at time and a half. What do you recommend that the hotel does?

4.2 The Leisure and Recreation Committee of Acornshire County Council have to consider closing a number of their facilities to remain within their reduced expenditure budget. One suggestion is to close one of the libraries. However, before making the decision the Chair of the Committee asks the Head of Library Services to provide the Committee with information on the number of people using the library. The Head of Library Services commissions a survey. The results are given in Table 6.21.

Use this information to write a briefing note for the Head of Library Services so that she may provide the Leisure and Recreation Committee with the information they require.

Table 6.21 Number of people using the library per day

2	2	33	25	20	15
3	2	50	38	44	33
12	9	6	5	37	28
4	3	33	25	28	21
6	5	6	5	22	17
34	26	18	14	51	38
7	5	17	13	41	31
5	4	15	11	27	20
27	20	33	25	38	29
6	5	45	34	4	3
15	11	27	20	16	12
3	2	49	37	22	17
11	8	18	14	12	32
10	8	14	11	15	24
9	7	37	28	5	6
6	5	8	6	24	11
31	23	18	14		

Chapter 7

Uncertainty in decision making I

The aims of this chapter are to introduce the ideas underpinning the concept of probability, and to use these ideas in a business context.
By the end of this chapter you should be able to:

- calculate the probability of certain events occurring, based on previous occurrences
- understand the link between probability and statistical frequencies
- combine probabilities
- calculate expected values for certain occurrences
- understand the limitations of probability as a tool for decision making.

- probability of an event occuring
- relative frequencies
- combinations of probabilities

Probability is concerned with future events and the likelihood of them occurring. Every day we make decisions based on probabilities. Leaving home in the morning without an umbrella, buying a lottery ticket, backing a horse, are all decisions based on probability. We weigh up, sometimes unconsciously, the probability that it is not going to rain, that we might win the jackpot, that the horse might win the race. These decisions are based on our previous experiences. It is exactly the same for businesses needing to make decisions about future events. A business may be considering launching a new product, entering a new market, possibly overseas, employing new staff, etc. All these are future events, and decisions need to be made about whether or not to go ahead.

Probability

The probability of an event occurring is a measure of how likely it is that the event will happen. Sometimes, we think of probability in terms of 'what is the chance of this happening?'

Example

A club sells 100 raffle tickets as a way of raising money for a local charity. You have bought one ticket. The chance that your ticket will be the winning ticket is 1 in 100, or 1/100. In other words, the probability that you have the winning ticket is 1/100 = 0.01. This can be expressed as:

p(you have the winning ticket) = 1/100 = 0.01

If you buy two of the 100 tickets you now have a 2 in 100 chance of winning

p(you have the winning ticket) = 2/100 = 0.02

This example demonstrates an *a priori* way of calculating a probability. We have been able to calculate the probability of an event happening (you have the winning ticket) before it happens, by using our knowledge of the situation.

In general, provided that all the outcomes are equally likely, the *a priori* probability is:

$$p \text{ (event)} = \frac{\text{Number of ways that event can occur}}{\text{Total number of possible outcomes}}$$

In the above example:

- The event is that you have the winning ticket.
- The number of ways that event can occur = 1, if you bought one ticket or 2, if you bought two tickets.
- The total number of possible outcomes = 100 as 100 tickets have been sold.

p(you have the winning ticket) = 1/100, if you bought one ticket
or p(you have the winning ticket) = 2/100, if you bought two tickets

If you bought all 100 tickets then you are bound to have the winning ticket, and:

p(you have the winning ticket) = 100/100 = 1

If you decided not to buy a ticket then you cannot win, and:

p(you have the winning ticket) = 0/100 = 0

Basic rules of probability

An event which is certain to happen has a probability of happening of one.
An event which cannot possibly happen has a probability of happening of zero.

Case Study

A market research agency employs 14 full-time researchers. Often there is more work than these 14 employees can manage, and the agency has to subcontract the work. Over the past year the agency has kept a record of the number of researchers needed each week. This data is given in Table 7.1. It is a simple ungrouped frequency table, showing the number of researchers required each week, and the number of weeks that the number of researchers were required.

Table 7.1 Market research agency demand for researchers

Number of researchers required x	Number of weeks f
10	1
11	5
12	10
13	17
14	8
15	5
16	4
	Total = 50 weeks

On 41 of the 50 weeks the agency could manage the work with its own staff, leaving nine weeks when some of the work had to be subcontracted. If this pattern of work continues next year, then again the agency would need to subcontract work for nine weeks out of 50, or for 18 per cent of weeks.

- What is the probability that the agency will have to subcontract work next week?
- What is the probability that the agency will not have to subcontract work next week?

In this case study we cannot use *a priori* probability. Instead we have to assume that the pattern of work next year will be the same as last year, and base the probabilities on last year's actual occurrences. We have estimated the probabilities using the **relative frequencies** of their occurrence. The relative frequency is calculated by dividing each value of the frequency in the frequency table by the total frequency.

The probability that the agency will need to subcontract work = 9/50 = 0.18
The probability that the agency will not need to subcontract work = 41/50 = 0.82

There are only these two options for the agency: either the work can be managed by their employees, or they need to subcontract. Add together the two probabilities:

p(agency does not subcontract) + p(agency subcontracts) = 0.82 + 0.18 = 1

Another basic rule of probability is that:

● The sum of the probabilities of all possible outcomes is ONE.

If the agency employed one more researcher, what is the probability that they will need to subcontract?

p(subcontract) = p(has work for more than 15 researchers) = 4/50 = 0.08
or p(subcontract) = 1 − p(has work for 15 or fewer researchers) = 1 − 46/50 = 1 − 0.92 = 0.08

A final packaging process is made up of two independent, but consecutive, machine operations: packing and addressing. Any packaging defects are removed from the process and do not reach the addressing operation. The packaging process produces 2 per cent defective packages, and the addressing 1 per cent defective addresses. What is the probability of an item entering the process being successfully packaged and addressed?

The simplest way of thinking this through is to imagine 100 items going through the operations.

● Of those 100 items, two will have defective packaging
● 98 will therefore be correctly packaged
● these 98 will then go on to be addressed
● of these 98 packages, 1 per cent will be incorrectly addressed
● 99 per cent of these 98 packages will be correctly addressed
● so 97 will be correctly packaged and addressed
● 97 out of the 100 original items will be correctly packaged and addressed.

The probability of an item entering the process being successfully packaged and addressed is therefore 0.97.

> While this may seem a longwinded way of finding a proba-
> bility, we shall see later that complicated probability cases can
> often be simplified if you use this method.

Activity 1

A small garage sells cars. Over the last year the owner has
recorded the number of cars sold each week. This is shown in
Table 7.2.

Table 7.2 Number of cars sold by the small garage

Number of cars sold per week	Number of weeks
0	12
1	14
2	8
3	6
4	6
5	4

If this pattern of sales continues, what is the probability that next week he sells:

1 no cars?
2 one car?
3 three or more cars?

Combining probabilities

The 'OR' rule

In Activity 1 you found the probability of selling three or more cars
by adding up the number of weeks that 3, 4 or 5 cars were sold and
dividing by 50, the number of weeks. This is an application of the
rule of addition of probabilities:

p(3 or more cars sold) =

$$\frac{\text{Number of weeks that 3, 4 or 5 cars were sold}}{\text{Total number of weeks}}$$

$$= \frac{6 + 6 + 4}{50}$$

= 16/50
= 0.32

This is the same as:

p(3 or 4 or 5 cars sold) = p(3 cars sold) + p(4 cars sold) + p(5 cars sold)
= 6/50 + 6/50 + 4/50 = 16/50 = 0.32

In general:

If A and B are two mutually exclusive events, then the probability of A or B occurring is:

p(A or B) =
$$\frac{\text{Number of ways A can happen} + \text{Number of ways B can happen}}{\text{Total number of possible outcomes}}$$

or p(A or B) = p(A) + p(B)

This formula only applies if two events A and B are **mutually exclusive**, that is, A and B cannot happen together.

If A and B can occur simultaneously then this formula double counts those occasions when this happens. In order to reach a general formula we must remove the double counting.

p(A or B) = p(A) + p(B) − p(A and B happen together)

The 'AND' rule

Here we are looking at the probability of two events both happening: p(A and B). This is often written as p(AB). We came across this in our second example, where we needed the probability that an item was correctly packaged and correctly addressed:

p(correct packaging and correct address) = p(correct packaging)× p(correct address)
= 0.98 × 0.99
= 0.97, the value we found earlier.

Example

In a production process four machines – a drill, a lathe, a grinder and a mill – all operate independently of each other. Their usage is:

● drill – 50 per cent
● lathe – 40 per cent
● grinder – 80 per cent
● mill – 70 per cent.

1. What is the probability that all the machines are busy at the same time?
p(drill is busy) = 0.5
p(lathe is busy) = 0.4
p(grinder is busy) = 0.8
p(mill is busy) = 0.7
As all the machines operate independently of each other the
p(all machines are busy)
= p(drill is busy AND lathe is busy AND grinder is busy AND mill is busy)
= p(drill is busy) × p(lathe is busy) × p(grinder is busy) × p(mill is busy)
= 0.5 × 0.4 × 0.8 × 0.7
= 0.112

2. What is the probability that both the drill and the lathe are idle at the same time?
= p(drill idle AND lathe idle)
= p(drill idle) × p(lathe idle)
= (1 − p(drill busy)) × (1− p(lathe busy))
= 0.5 × 0.6
= 0.3

3. What is the probability that all the machines are idle at the same time?
= p(drill idle AND lathe idle AND mill idle AND grinder idle)
= p(drill idle) × p(lathe idle) × p(mill idle) × p(grinder idle)
= (1 − p(drill busy)) × (1 − p(lathe busy)) × (1 − p(mill busy)) × (1 − p(grinder busy))
= 0.5 × 0.6 × 0.3 × 0.2
= 0.018

Example

Pearshaped Computers use Gizmo Electronics' switches in the manufacture of their personal computers. Each switch has a probability of failure of 0.01, but this is totally independent of all other switches. A personal computer will fail if at least half of the switches fail. What is the probability that:

1 A two-switch personal computer will fail?
2 A four-switch personal computer will fail?

1. A two-switch personal computer will fail if more than half of the switches fail, in other words if both switches fail. (Remembering the 'AND' rule of probability: 'AND' signifies multiply the probabilities.) The probability that a two-switch personal computer will fail:
= p(first switch fails AND second switch fails)
= p(first switch fails) × p(second switch fails)
= 0.01 × 0.01
= 0.0001

2. A four-switch personal computer will fail if more than half of the switches fail, in other words if three switches fail, or if four switches fail. (Remembering the 'OR' rule of probability: 'OR' signifies add the probabilities.) The probability that a four-switch personal computer will fail:
= p(3 switches fail OR 4 switches fail)
= p(3 switches fail) + p(4 switches fail)

(a) p(4 switches fail) = p(all 4 switches fail)
(The 'AND' rule again)

$$= 0.01 \times 0.01 \times 0.01 \times 0.01$$
$$= 0.00000001$$

(b) p(3 switches fail) =
(The 'AND' and 'OR' rules both apply here)

p(1st switch OK AND other 3 fail)
or p(2nd switch OK AND other 3 fail)
or p (3rd switch OK AND other 3 fail)
or p (4th switch OK AND other 3 fail)
p(3 switches fail) = $0.01^3 \times 0.99 + 0.01^3 \times 0.99 + 0.01^3 \times 0.99 + 0.01^3 \times 0.99$
$= 4 \times 0.01^3 \times 0.99$
$= 0.00000396$

Case Study

The Market Research Company is bidding for a new contract, which will keep two researchers fully employed for the next 50 weeks. The managing director assesses the probability of winning the new contract as being between 0.6 and 0.75.

If they win the contract, the managing director will need to review the number of researchers employed, and possibly employ another one, or two, on short-term contracts. There seem to be a lot of uncertainties, and the managing director is seeking clarification.

As a first step, list the options:

● win contract
● do not employ new researcher, and subcontract work as necessary
● employ one more researcher on fixed term contract, and subcontract work as necessary
● employ two more researchers on fixed term contracts, and subcontract work as necessary.

There are probabilities associated with all of these options. Once these are known, the managing director can assign costs to the various options and make decisions. (This is covered later in this chapter.)

Of course, we have to assume that, in addition to the new contract, the existing pattern of work still continues. First of all, there is a range of values for the probability of winning the contract (between 0.6 and 0.75). We can work through the options first at a probability of 0.6 and secondly, at a probability of 0.75.

p(winning) = 0.6
Option: do not employ new researcher, and subcontract work as necessary. If the existing pattern of work still continues, there will be work for two more researchers, and the company will have to subcontract when there is work for 13,14,15 or 16 researchers.

p(winning contract and subcontracting) = p(winning) × p(subcontracting)
= 0.6 × p(work for 13, or 14, or 15, or 16 researchers)
= 0.6 × (17 + 8 + 5 + 4)/50
= 0.6 × 34/50
= 0.6 × 0.68
= 0.408

Case Study Exercise 1

Find the probabilities associated with:

1 all the other options
2 with p(winning) = 0.75

Combining probabilities when the events are not mutually exclusive

So far we have only combined probabilities relating to mutually exclusive events, but this is not always the case. This was very briefly mentioned under the earlier section on the 'OR rule':

If A and B are two events which can occur simultaneously then the simple p(A + B) = p(A) + p(B) formula double counts those occasions when this happens.

In order to reach a general formula we must remove the double counting.

p(A or B) = p(A) + p(B) − p(A and B happen together)
= p(A) + p(B) − p(AB)

Consider the following: a representative of the work force is being selected to meet an important visitor for lunch. Fifty members of the workforce have indicated that they would like to be considered. Of these, 30 are women and 20 are men; 15 work on the production line, 25 in sales and the rest in finance. What is the probability that the worker selected will be either a woman or from sales?

If we applied the simple 'OR rule' here:

p(woman or sales) = p(woman) + p(sales)
= 0.6 + 0.5 = 1.1

This is clearly wrong, as the answer is more than one. We have double counted the women in sales.

The probability: p(woman or sales) should be:

p(woman or sales) = p(woman) + p(sales) − p(woman and sales)
= 1.1 − (p(woman) × p(sales))
= 1.1 − 0.6 × 0.5 = 1.1 − 0.3 = 0.8

If we change the scenario slightly; so that two members of staff are to be selected. What is the probability that both selected staff are from sales? Thinking about this, these two events are not independent. The second probability depends on the first.

p(first is from sales) = 25/50 = 0.5

Now that this person has been selected there are only 49 left to choose from, and, if this person is from sales, only 24 come from sales.

p(second is from sales given the first is from sales) = 24/49

This is called a **conditional probability.**

A **conditional probability** is the probability that event B will occur, given that event A has already occurred. It is written as: p(B/A).

In this case: p(B/A) is the probability that the second selected is from sales, given that the first selected is from sales.

The 'AND rule' for events which are not independent is:

p(A and B) = p(A) × p(A/B)

Probability trees

Sometimes probabilities can become difficult to calculate, particularly if there are several events whose outcomes depend on the outcomes of other events. On these occasions it can be useful to draw a **probability tree** illustrating the possible outcomes, and replace the probabilities by the number of occasions out of 100 that these events could happen.

Example

A regular commuter drives from home to the station and catches a train to work. Occasionally she leaves home late in the morning, sometimes the traffic can be unusually heavy and she can miss the train, once she has caught the train it can also be late arriving at her destination. Knowing the probabilities of the various events, which are all interconnected, she can calculate the probability of being late for work.

Past experience indicates the following probabilities:

p(leaves home late) = 0.25
p(traffic heavy so she misses the train) = 0.5
p(train arrives late at the destination) = 0.2

Rather than work with all the possible combined probabilities, imagine 100 typical journeys to work. On 75 occasions she leaves home on time and on 25 she leaves late. Irrespective of the time she left home, the traffic can be heavy 50 per cent of the time, and she will miss the train and so on.

   The events and the number of occasions, out of 100 journeys, can be drawn as a probability tree, as shown in Figure 7.1.

   There are four different points on the probability tree where the outcome is 'late for work'. These account for 37.5 + 12.5 + 7.5 + 2.5 = 60 occasions out of the 100 journeys, giving a probability of being late for work of 60/100 = 0.6.

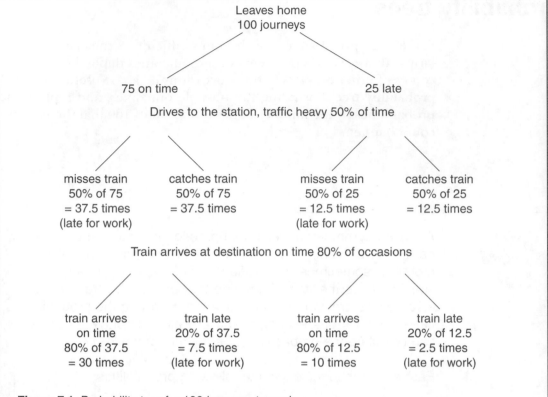

Figure 7.1 Probability tree for 100 journeys to work

Activity 2

The four machines used in the production process described in an earlier example all operate independently of each other. The process is that products always go through the machines in the following order:

1 drill
2 lathe
3 grinder
4 mill.

Each machine occasionally produces defective items, and so the quality of the items
is checked at each stage. Any defective items found are taken out of production and
either scrapped or reworked. Past experience shows that the probability of a defective item produced at each machine is:

1 drill = 0.01
2 lathe = 0.02
3 grinder = 0.02
4 mill = 0.025

What is the probability of the production of a satisfactory product?

Expected values

Returning to our first example where a club sells 100 raffle tickets as
a way of raising money for a local charity, the tickets cost £2 each and
the prize is £150. You really want to know if it is worth paying £2 to
buy the ticket, as the probability of winning is only 0.01.

Expected values link probability with money invested and money
returned. If the club ran 100 raffles each exactly the same, then you
would expect to win one raffle. Your winnings would be £150, but
your outlay would be 100 tickets at £2 each, i.e. £200. This is £50
more than the winnings, so it is not really worth while buying the 100
tickets.

The **expected value** of the raffle is a loss of £50, on 100 raffles. The
expected value of the one raffle is a loss of £50/100, i.e. 50 pence.

This can be derived directly using the probabilities:

p(winning) = 0.01   value of winning = £150 − cost of ticket
p(losing) = 0.99   value of losing = loss of cost of ticket
expected value = value of winning × p(winning) + value of losing ×
p(losing)
= (£150 − cost of ticket) × 0.01 + (loss of cost of ticket) × 0.99
= 148 × 0.01 − 2 × 0.99
= −50 pence

Activity 3

How much would you be prepared to pay for one of these 100 raffle tickets?

Remember

In general:

Expected value = Σ(probability of outcome) × (value of outcome)

Example

The number of television sets sold each day at a discount store, and the probability of selling that number of sets, are given in Table 7.3. Calculate the expected number of television sets sold per day.

Table 7.3 Number of television sets sold

Number of TV sets sold X	Probability of selling that number $p(X=x)$
0	0.516
1	0.258
2	0.129
3	0.065
4	0.032

The expected values are found by multiplying the number of sets sold, *x*, by the probability of that number of sets being sold. These values are shown in Table 7.4. They are then totalled to give the expected value.

Table 7.4 Number of television sets sold

| Number of TV sets sold | Probability of selling that number | |
x	p	x × p
0	0.516	0
1	0.258	0.258
2	0.129	0.258
3	0.065	0.195
4	0.032	0.128
Total =	1.00	0.839

The expected number of sets sold per day = 0.839. Clearly the store will not sell 0.839 sets on any one day, but over a period of time the store will expect to sell 0.839 sets per day. Note: this is the mean number of television sets sold each day. This can be checked by replacing the probabilities used by the frequencies (based on, for example, 100 days) and finding the mean number of sets sold.

The expected value is, in fact, the mean, demonstrating the link between probabilities and frequency tables.

This is also shown in the following example, where the data is presented in a frequency table, the frequencies are then converted to probabilities. The expected number of hours to be worked per week next year is then calculated using the probabilities.

A table such as Table 7.3, showing the probabilities of occurrence for each possible value (or range of values) of the variable is called a **probability distribution**. The sum of all the probabilities in the probability distribution is one.

Example

A freelance IT consultant has a portfolio of organizations for whom she works. Last year she worked 50 weeks, however, the hours varied each week. She has recorded the number of hours she worked each week for those 50 weeks; these are shown in Table 7.5.

Table 7.5 Hours worked by IT consultant

Hours per week	Number of weeks
0–9 inclusive	8
10–19 inclusive	12
20–29 inclusive	15
30–39 inclusive	13
40–49 inclusive	2
Total =	50

She intends to charge £70 per hour for all future work, but does not expect the pattern of work to change. Calculate her expected weekly income for the forthcoming year.

The hours worked per week are recorded in classes. The mid-point of each class is used in the calculations, exactly as before (see Chapter 6 – Calculating the mean from a frequency table).

The probability of working those hours each week is taken to be the relative frequency of working those hours, i.e. divide each individual frequency by 50, the total number of weeks worked. Both these sets of figures are tabulated and shown in Table 7.6.

Table 7.6 Hours worked by IT consultant

Hours per week	Number of weeks	p(working those hours)	Hours per week mid-point	p × mid-point
0–9 inclusive	8	0.16	4.5	0.72
10–19 inclusive	12	0.24	14.5	3.48
20–29 inclusive	15	0.3	24.5	7.35
30–39 inclusive	13	0.26	34.5	8.97
40–49 inclusive	2	0.04	44.5	1.78
Total =	50	1Mean hours per week =		22.3

The expected number of hours to be worked each week = 22.3. The hourly rate is £70 per hour, giving an expected weekly income of £1561. (While there is no change in the work pattern the expected number of hours for next year will be the mean number of hours worked this year.)

Case Study

In order to make meaningful decisions, the managing director really needs to be able to put monetary values to each of the options being considered. Each permanent researcher costs the agency £400 per day. The cost of subcontracting the work costs £800 per researcher, per day. What is the cost per day, before the agency bids for the new contract?

The cost of the 14 permanent researchers = £400 × 14 = £5600 per day. This cost is incurred regardless of the amount of work.

Earlier we found that the agency could manage with the permanent researchers on 41 days out of 50, on five days there was sufficient work for one subcontractor, and on four days there was work for two subcontractors.

The probabilities and extra costs are:

- p(subcontract one researcher) = 5/50 = 0.1 extra cost £800
- p(subcontract two researchers) = 4/50 = 0.08 extra cost £1600

The expected cost = £5600 + 0.1 × £800 + 0.08 × £1600
= £5600 + £80 + £128
= £5808 per day

Case Study Exercise 2

🖫
The managing director now wants to know how many permanent researchers should be employed so that, in the long run, the expected cost is at a minimum. By considering different combinations of permanent researchers and subcontractors, calculate this number of permanent researchers.

Summary

In this chapter we looked at uncertainty in business decision making. There are many situations where a business can use expected values to assist in choosing between different options.

Probability can appear difficult at first, and the topic often needs to be taken steadily. Working through examples and activities will help.

We covered the basic rules of probability: the AND and OR rules, sometimes referred to as the rules of addition and multiplication. These rules form the foundation of decision theory.

Further reading

Morris, C. (1996). A firm foundation: elementary probability in *Quantitative Approaches in Business Studies*. Pitman Publishing.

1. Multiple choice

1.1 A commuter catches the 08.15 train from his local station every weekday. During the last 12 weeks, it was on time on 12 occasions, late on 42 occasions and early on four occasions, and twice it did not run. From this information the probability that tomorrow the train will be:

(a) late   (d) it will not be on time
(b) on time   (e) it will run
(c) will not run
is:
A 2/42   F 12/60
B 2/60   G 14/60
C 12/42   H 48/60
D 42/60   I 58/60
E 2/12   J 38/42

1.2 Which of the following events are mutually exclusive?
(a) Living in Sussex and working in London
(b) The sun is shining and it is raining
(c) Being male and having red hair
(d) The same horse coming first and third in one race
(e) Winning the lottery and winning the pools

2. Explain the meaning of the following:
2.1 Independent events
2.2 Mutually exclusive events
2.3 Conditional probability
2.4 Expected value

3. Calculate the following probabilities:
3.1 Mr Baptiste can either walk to work, or take the bus, or drive his car. The probability that Mr Baptiste walks to work is 0.15, and the probability that he takes the bus is 0.2. What is the probability that on a given day he will drive to work?
3.2 Two machines operate in a workshop. The probability that machine A will last for another four years is 0.2, while the prob-

ability that machine B will last for another four years is 0.25. Find the probability that:

(a) Both machines will be operating in four years' time.

(b) Neither machine will be operating in four years' time.

(c) At least one machine will be operating in four years' time.

3.3 An electronic timer is made from six components; two of component A, two of B and two of C. The components are delivered in large boxes. In the past, 5 per cent of component A, 2 per cent of component B and 10 per cent of component C have been found to be defective. The timer will only work if all its component parts are without defect.

(a) What proportion of timers will work?

(b) What proportion of timers will not work?

(c) A customer buys a pack of three timers; what is the probability that exactly one timer does not work?

3.4 A piece of equipment will only function if three components A, B, and C are all working. The probability of A failing during the first year of operation is 0.05, that of B failing is 0.15 and that of C failing is 0.1. What is the probability that the equipment will fail before the end of the first year?

3.5 Components arrive in bulk in containers at a factory. Past experience shows that 5 per cent of these components are defective. Before the consignment is accepted, five of these components are selected for testing. What is the probability that of these five components:

(a) No defective component will be found?

(b) There will be exactly one defective component?

(c) There will be exactly two defective components?

4. Case study

The Elms is a large garden centre, selling a range of plants. The manager, Mrs Mandel, buys most of the plants from a local nursery, but is considering diversifying by growing the plants from seed herself. The head gardener considers that growing the plants from seed can be a risky business; there is no guarantee that the seeds will germinate or, if they do germinate, they may not survive and grow.

Mrs Mandel asks the head gardener to assess the risks at each stage in the process of producing plants from seed. This he does, and presents her with the following information:

● The chance of a seed germinating is 85 per cent.
● The plants are then transplanted three times into bigger pots. At each transplantation there is a 10 per cent chance that the plant will die.

● Finally, the plants are packaged for sale, where there is a 5 per cent chance that the plant will not survive.

While she finds this interesting, Mrs Mandel really wants to know the probability that a seed will survive the whole process, not just the individual stages. She has a large order for 200 plants, and is unsure of how many seeds to plant to be sure of meeting the order. Advise her.

The local council has decided to enter the 'Britain in Bloom' competition and needs to buy a large quantity of geraniums to plant in the hanging baskets which will adorn the lampposts in the town. Mrs Mandel is keen to supply the geraniums, but does not have sufficient plants on order from the local nursery. She has three alternatives:

1 Ask the head gardener to grow the geraniums.
2 Buy extra geraniums from the local nursery.
3 Buy the geraniums from a supplier in Holland.

The problem is that each of these alternatives has different costs and benefits associated with it. Asking the head gardener to grow the geraniums will require major investment in a new glasshouse and equipment. Mrs Mandel feels that such an investment will only be cost effective if the council order is sufficiently large. Buying from the local nursery will be safer if the order is not large, as she need only buy the quantity required. Buying from a Dutch nursery offers good quality plants, but with a risk of disruption in supply.

At present Mrs Mandel does not know the size of the order, so she thinks she will work on three scenarios: a small order, a medium order and a large order. She assesses the probability of a small order as 0.2, that of a medium order as 0.5 and a large order as 0.3. She then looks at the associated profits the garden centre could make for the three alternatives against the three scenarios. This information is given in Table 7.7.

Table 7.7 Contribution to profit of each alternative

Alternative sources of geraniums	Size of order (£000s)		
	small	medium	large
1. Head gardener	−10	15	45
2. Order from local nursery	5	25	30
3. Order from Holland	10	30	25

By looking at the expected values of each of the three alternatives,

Chapter 8

Uncertainty in decision making II

The aim of this chapter is to continue to explore the concept of uncertainty in the business world, which was started in Chapter 7, and to use a particular probability distribution – the normal distribution – as a business decision-making tool.

By the end of this chapter you will be able to:

Aims

- recognize situations where the use of the normal distribution is appropriate
- use normal distribution tables to solve problems arising from such situations.

Key Concepts

- probability distributions
- standardized normal distribution

- Z values
- normal distribution tables

Introduction

The normal distribution is a probability distribution which frequently occurs in business situations. Typical examples of normal distributions can involve measurements, such as weight, length, volume etc.

It is a symmetrical distribution, which means that the mean, median and mode coincide at the centre.

This chapter will build on many of the statistical topics already covered. In particular probability, frequency/probability tables, means and standard deviations. If you are unsure about any of these topics, it would be wise to refresh your memory before starting on this chapter.

Case Study

A supermarket buys its 'own brand' coffee from Ember Coffee Supplies Ltd. The 100-gram jars of speciality Colombian coffee are particularly popular with the customers. However, recently the supermarket has received some complaints from its customers that some of the jars seem to be underweight. The chief buyer discusses the problem with Mr Lee, Ember's production manager.

The jars are filled automatically, by machine, but there is always a certain amount of variation in the weight of the contents. Mr Lee had set the machine to fill the jars with slightly more than 100 grams, but there is a possibility that the machine is set too low, and that some may contain fewer than 100 grams.

Mr Lee decides to accurately weigh a sample of the jars. He weighs the contents of 1000 randomly selected jars and constructs a frequency table, Table 8.1, and draws a histogram, Figure 8.1, showing these weights.

As the machine has been set to put slightly more than 100 grams in each jar, the middle of the distribution is not at 100 grams, but seems to lie between 102 and 104 grams.

The histogram is fairly symmetrical about this middle class, with about the same number of jars above and below. The majority of jars are in the middle of the distribution. The further from the middle, the fewer jars. However, some jars certainly contain fewer than 100 grams.

Table 8.1 Frequency table showing the weights of 1000 jars of coffee

Weight (g)	Number of packs
96 and under 98	7
98 and under 100	65
100 and under 102	228
102 and under 104	302
104 and under 106	237
106 and under 108	84
108 and under 110	69
110 and under 112	8
Total =	1000

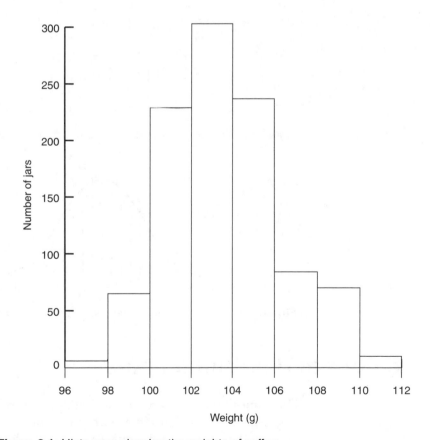

Figure 8.1 Histogram showing the weights of coffee

*Case Study
Exercise 1*

As a revision exercise calculate the mean and standard deviation for this set of data. (These statistics will be needed later in the case study.)

If Mr Lee had made the classes smaller, as shown in Figure 8.2, the histogram is smoother. Further reduction in class size along with more data would have made the histogram even smoother, until the histogram closely approximates to a smooth curve, as shown in Figure 8.3. This smooth curve is a **normal distribution curve**.

Figure 8.2 Histogram showing the weights of the jars using smaller classes

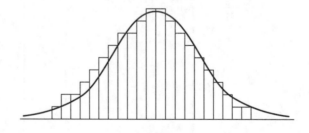

Figure 8.3 Histogram with normal distribution curve superimposed

The normal distribution curve

The smooth curve shown in Figure 8.3 is a normal distribution curve. It is also shown in Figure 8.4, without being superimposed on the histogram. The curve represents a theoretical distribution: the normal distribution. It is a bell-shaped, symmetrical curve. The line of symmetry is at the point where the mean, median and mode all coincide.

The two halves either side of this line are mirror images of each other.

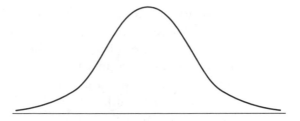

Figure 8.4 The normal distribution curve

If an actual distribution displays similar properties to these, then the theoretical distribution can be used in its place as a tool for further analysis. However, we need to know the actual mean and standard deviation. These two statistics define the appropriate normal distribution. There are as many normal distributions as there are possible combinations of means and standard deviations. All the curves have the same basic shape, but their position along the x-axis varies according to the mean and their spread varies according to the standard deviation. Figure 8.5 shows three different normal distribution curves. Two have the same mean, but different spreads (standard deviations), and two have different means, but the same spread (standard deviation).

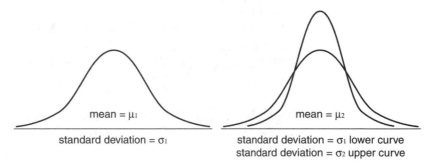

mean = μ_1

standard deviation = σ_1

mean = μ_2

standard deviation = σ_1 lower curve
standard deviation = σ_2 upper curve

Figure 8.5 Three normal distribution curves with different means and standard deviations

There is one major difference between the theoretical and the actual distributions: the normal distribution curve never actually crosses the x-axis, it is asymptotic to it. In other words there is no minimum or maximum value to the theoretical distribution. Of course, the actual distribution has minimum and maximum values.

The theoretical distribution allows for the possibility, however remote, of a value being bigger, or smaller than we have come across so far.

You will remember that, when looking at a histogram, the **frequency is represented by the area of the rectangles**, not the heights. Similarly for the normal distribution curve, **the frequency is represented by the area under the curve**, not the height of the curve. In the last chapter we also looked at the link between frequency and probability. This link tells us that the probability is also represented by the **area under the curve**.

Properties of the normal distribution:

1 a symmetrical distribution
2 bell shaped
3 the mean = the median = the mode
4 the frequencies (and hence the probabilities) are represented by the area under the curve
5 50 per cent of all possible observations are above the mean and 50 per cent below (this follows from points (1) and (3)).

The normal distribution also has other properties, which make it a useful business tool. The most important of these are the following, and hold for any combination of mean and standard deviation:

1 68.26 per cent of the distribution lies within ±1 standard deviation of the mean
2 95.45 per cent of the distribution lies within ±2 standard deviations of the mean
3 99.74 per cent of the distribution lies within ± 3 standard deviations of the mean.

Returning to the case study where the mean = 103.53 and the standard deviation = 2.69. The theoretical distribution tells us that:

1 68.26 per cent of the distribution lies within ±1 standard deviation of the mean i.e. between 103.53 − 2.69 = 100.84 and 103.53 + 2.69 = 106.22
2 95.45 per cent of the distribution lies within ±2 standard deviations of the mean i.e. between 103.53 − 2 × 2.69 = 98.15 and 103.53 + 2 × 2.69 = 108.91
3 99.74 per cent of the distribution lies within ±3 standard deviations of the mean i.e. between 103.53 − 3 × 2.69 = 95.46 and 103.53 + 3 × 2.69 = 111.60

*Case Study
Exercise 2*

Using the 1000 weights collected by Mr Lee, find out how many
of the 1000 actually fell in these ranges.

It is unlikely that anyone will remember these exact percentages,
and they are only a selection. We may also want to know how many
observations fall in a different range, or the probability that an
observation will fall in a particular range. Luckily all these values are
tabulated for us, and are available on Excel.

However, we have already seen that there are many different normal distributions, each with its own mean and standard deviation. It
would not be possible to produce a set of tables for every possible
combination of mean and standard deviation.

Since all normal distributions have the same features they can all
be converted to one **standard normal distribution**.

The standard normal distribution

We have already seen that the normal distribution can be considered
to be a family of distributions, each distribution being defined by its
mean (μ) and standard deviation (σ).

The standard normal distribution is defined as the normal distribution with

● a mean equal to zero
● a standard deviation equal to one
● the total area under the standard normal curve is one.

A variable having a standard normal distribution is given the letter z,
in order to distinguish it from other variables (usually given the letters x and y).

Use of standard normal tables

The probabilities associated with the standard normal distribution
(i.e. the areas under the standard normal curve) are tabulated in
Appendix A. From this table we can read off the probability that z is
greater than a particular value. This probability is shown as the shad-

ed area in Figure 8.6. It also appears as a reminder at the top of the standard normal table. It is sometimes referred to as the area in the tail of the distribution, and again this appears, as a reminder, at the top of the standard normal table.

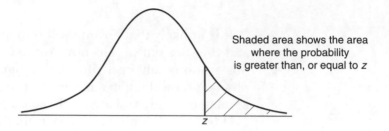

Figure 8.6 Standard normal distribution curve showing area under the curve

As an example in how to use the table, we can look up the probability that z is greater than, or equal to, two. This will be the proportion of observations in the standard normal distribution greater than, or equal to, two standard deviations from the mean, and is the shaded area in Figure 8.7.

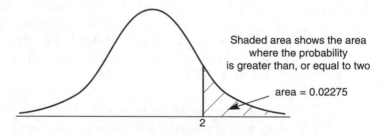

Figure 8.7 Standard normal distribution showing two standards deviations from the mean

Turn to Appendix A and look down the left-hand side of the tables (the z column) for $z = 2.0$, then read off the figure in the 0.00 column. This is 0.02275. This tells us that the shaded area in Figure 8.7 is 0.02275. Remember that the whole area under the curve is one.

Using this, the probability that z is less than, or equal to 2 – the shaded area shown in Figure 8.8 – subtract 0.02275 from one giving 0.97725.

Hint: roughly sketch a normal distribution curve and shade the area representing the probability you are seeking, then compare this sketch with the sketch at the top of the tables.

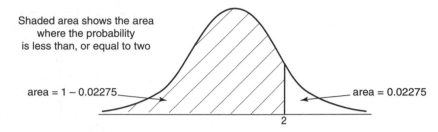

Figure 8.8 Standard normal distribution showing area where the probability is less than or equal to two

Further examples using the tables:

1 *If the value of z has two decimal places*
   To obtain the probability that z is greater than, or equal to, 2.05:
   – look down the z column in the tables for $z = 2.0$
   – then move along this row to the column headed 0.05
   – read off this value
   – the probability is 0.02018
   The area is illustrated in Figure 8.9.

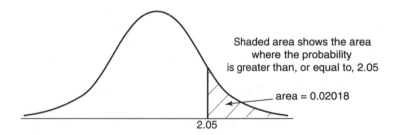

Figure 8.9 Normal curve with $z = 2.05$

2 *If the probability required is between 0 and a particular value*
   To obtain the probability that z is between 0 and 1.25. This can be written as $p(0 \leqslant z \leqslant 1.25)$ and is shown as the shaded area in Figure 8.10.
   If we look up $z = 1.25$ in the normal distribution tables we get 0.1056. This is the probability that z is greater than or equal to 1.25 i.e. $p(z \geqslant 1.25) = 0.1056$.
   Compare the shaded area in Figure 8.10 with the shaded area on the curve at the top of the tables. Since all normal distribution curves are symmetrical about the mean (=median) and each half is a mirror image of the other then: the $p(z \geqslant 0) = 0.5$, so that $p(0 \leqslant z \leqslant 1.25) = 0.5 - 0.1056 = 0.3944$.

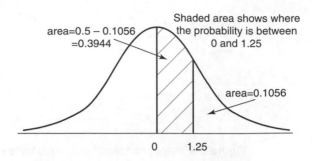

Figure 8.10 Normal curve where p(0 ⩽ z ⩽1.25) is shown

3 *If the probability required is less than a particular value of z*
To obtain the probability that z is less than, or equal to, 1.25, we subtract 0.1056 from 1.
p(z ⩽ 1.25) ≑ 1 – 0.1056 = 0.8944 (see Figure 8.11).

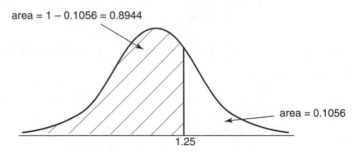

Figure 8.11 Normal curve where p(z ⩽ 1.25) is shown

4 *If z is a negative number*
To obtain the probability that z is less than –1.5, i.e. p(z ⩽ –1.5) (see Figure 8.12).

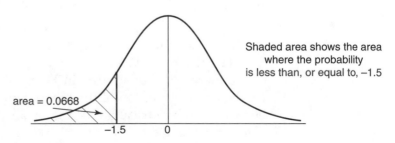

Figure 8.12 Normal curve with z = –1.5

You will have noticed that there are no negative values in the table of areas under the standard normal curve. This is because all normal distribution curves are symmetrical about the mean, the two halves are mirror images of each other, and $p(z \leqslant -1.5) = p(z \geqslant +1.5) = 0.0668$.

Activity 1

🖫

Use the standard normal tables to find the following probabilities:

1   $p(z \geqslant 1.2)$
2   $p(0 \leqslant z \leqslant 1.2)$
3   $p(z \leqslant 1.97)$
4   $p(z \geqslant -1.6)$
5   $p(1.1 \leqslant z \leqslant 1.8)$

Conversion to a standard normal distribution

Now that you are familiar with the use of the normal distribution tables, you are probably wondering how this standard normal curve relates to a real normal distribution curve, whose mean and standard deviation are not 1 and 0 respectively. In particular, how will the standard normal curve help Mr Lee, where the mean is 103.53 and the standard deviation is 2.69?

Earlier, we saw that all normal distribution curves have the same basic shape, but their position along the x-axis varies according to the mean and their spread varies according to the standard deviation. This is illustrated in Figure 8.5 – three different normal distribution curves; two with the same mean, but different spreads (standard deviations), and two with different means, but the same spread (standard deviation).

If the first of these curves has a mean of 10 and a standard deviation of 2, then

● mean plus 1 standard deviation = 12
● mean plus 2 standard deviations = 14
● mean plus 3 standard deviations = 16
● mean minus 1 standard deviation = 8
● mean minus 2 standard deviations = 6

● mean minus 3 standard deviations = 4

Figure 8.13 compares this normal distribution curve with the standard normal curve. On each curve the points:

● mean (10 and 0)
● mean ± 1 standard deviation (12 and 1, and, 8 and –1),
● mean ± 2 standard deviations (14 and 2, and 6 and –2),
● mean ± 3 standard deviations (16 and 3, and 4 and –3),

correspond.

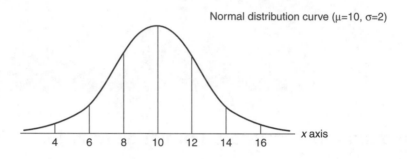

Normal distribution curve (μ=10, σ=2)

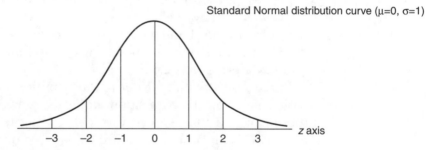

Standard Normal distribution curve (μ=0, σ=1)

Figure 8.13 Comparison between a normal distribution curve ($\mu = 10$, $\sigma = 2$) and the standard normal distribution curve ($\mu = 0$, $\sigma = 1$)

The conversion which makes these points correspond is:

1 subtract the mean
2 divide by the standard deviation.

These two steps convert any point (x) from a normal distribution curve to the corresponding point (z) on the standard normal distribution. The formula for this conversion can be expressed as:

$$z = \frac{x - \mu}{\sigma}$$

Select one point at random, e.g. $x = 11$, from our normal distribution curve and see what point, z, this corresponds to on the standard normal distribution curve. This is shown on Figure 8.14, where z can be seen to be between 0 and 1 on the standard normal distribution curve.

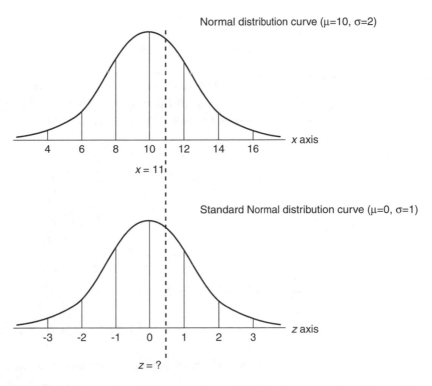

Figure 8.14 Comparison between a normal distribution curve ($\mu = 10$, $\sigma = 2$) and the standard normal distribution curve ($\mu = 0$, $\sigma = 1$)

Applying the two step conversion we get:

1 subtract the mean from x: $11 - 10 = 1$
2 divide by the standard deviation: $1/2 = 0.5$

therefore $z = 0.5$

If the value of *x* is less than its mean, then the value of *z* will be negative.

Light bulbs manufactured by Gable Lights plc are expected to last 200 hours. In fact, past experience indicates that the lifetime of the bulbs follows a normal distribution with a mean of 200 hours and a standard deviation of 4 hours. Calculate the probability that a randomly selected bulb will last:

(a) at least 206 hours
(b) less than 198 hours
(c) between 204 and 208 hours.

In each of these we shall need to convert our normal distribution with $\mu = 200$ and $\sigma = 4$ to the standard normal distribution, and then use normal distribution tables.

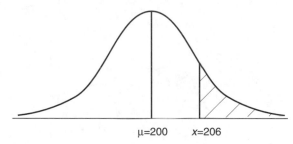

μ=200   *x*=206

Figure 8.15 Gable Lights plc (a)

(a) Here we require p($x \geqslant 206$), this is the shaded area on Figure 8.15.
   (i) Apply the conversion to get the *z* value corresponding to
       x = 206

$$z = \frac{x - \mu}{\sigma}$$

$$z = \frac{206 - 200}{4}$$

$$z = 6/4 = 1.5$$

   (ii) Use the normal distribution tables (or the Excel function) to get the probability p($z \geqslant 1.5$). As before, compare the shaded area on Figure 8.15 with the shaded area at the top of the tables.

p($z \geqslant 1.5$) = 0.0668

Therefore the probability that a bulb selected at random will last at least 206 hours is 0.0668.

(b) Here we require p($x \leqslant 198$), this is the shaded area on Figure 8.16.

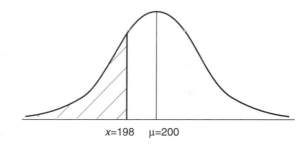

x=198 μ=200

Figure 8.16 Gable Lights plc (b)

(i) The conversion to get the z value corresponding to $x = 198$ gives:

$$z = \frac{x - \mu}{\sigma}$$

$$z = \frac{198 - 200}{4}$$

$$z = -2/4 = -0.5$$

(ii) Use the normal distribution tables (or the Excel function) to get the probability p($z \leqslant -0.5$). As before, compare the shaded area on Figure 8.16 with the shaded area at the top of the tables. The opposite 'tails' are shaded, but as the normal distribution curve is symmetrical the areas will be equal.

p($z \leqslant -0.5$) = 0.3085

Therefore the probability that a bulb selected at random will last less than 198 hours is 0.3085.

(c) We require the probability that a bulb will last between 204 and 208 hours, i.e. $p(204 \leqslant x \leqslant 208)$.
This is shown on Figure 8.17.

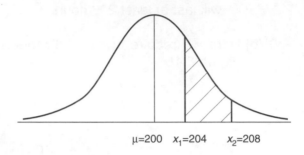

$\mu=200$ $x_1=204$ $x_2=208$

Figure 8.17 Gable Lights plc (c)

(i) Here there are two values of x (204 and 208) to be converted to z values:

$$z_1 = \frac{204 - 200}{4} \qquad\qquad z_2 = \frac{208 - 200}{4}$$

$$z_1 = 4/4 = 1 \qquad\qquad z_2 = 8/4 = 2$$

(ii) Using normal distribution tables $p(z \geqslant 1) = 0.1587$ and $p(z \geqslant 2) = 0.02275$. Subtracting the two probabilities gives:

$$p(1 \leqslant z \leqslant 2) = 0.13595$$

Therefore, the probability that a bulb will last between 204 and 208 hours is 0.13595.

Activity 2

The length of women's feet follows a normal distribution with a mean of 25 cm and a standard deviation of 2 cm. A manufacturer of women's shoes makes 100 000 pairs of each of the most popular styles each year. To help the company plan the production, how many of the 100 000 pairs should be:

(a) at least 28 cm?
(b) less than 21.5 cm?
(c) between 23 and 27 cm?

Case Study

By accurately weighing the contents of 1000 jars of coffee, Mr Lee has established that the automatic filling machine fills with a mean of 103.53 grams and a standard deviation of 2.69 grams. The distribution of weights appears to follow a normal distribution, and he decides to use this to find the probability that a jar selected at random will contain fewer than 100 grams.

He draws a rough sketch of the normal distribution curve (Figure 8.18) and marks the mean and 100 grams on it. He realizes from this sketch that he needs to convert 100 grams to a z statistic, then use normal distribution tables.

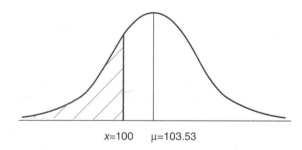

$x=100$ $\mu=103.53$

Figure 8.18 Normal distribution with the mean of 103.53 g and 100 g marked

$$z = \frac{100 - 103.53}{2.69}$$

$$z = -3.53/2.69 = -1.31$$

The value of z is negative, but as all normal distribution curves are symmetrical, he knows that the areas in the two 'tails' are the same.

To find the probability he looks up $z = 1.31$ in the tables. This gives $p(z \leqslant -1.31) = 0.0951$. Therefore the probability that a jar selected at random contains fewer than 100 grams is 0.0951, or 9.5 per cent.

He reports this figure to the supermarket buyer, who considers it is too high, and wants it reduced to 1 per cent.

Mr Lee, anxious to keep the contract, agrees but is not sure what to do. He knows that he must increase the mean setting on the automatic filling machine, but what should this new mean be?

Let's look at how the normal distribution can help Mr Lee calculate the new mean so that no more than 1 per cent of jars contain fewer than 100 g. Figure 8.19 illustrates this.

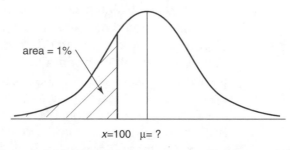

Figure 8.19 Normal distribution showing one per cent of jars containing fewer than 100 g

Mr Lee knows the probability (0.01), and therefore the area in the tail of the normal distribution must be 0.01, but he does not know the mean. We are going to assume that changing the mean setting on the filling machine does not affect the standard deviation.

Mr Lee's problem is, in fact, the reverse of the normal distribution problems we solved earlier in the chapter. It is solved in the reverse order to the earlier problems, but using Appendix B, which gives the z value corresponding to a known area in the tail of the distribution, instead of Appendix A. (If you are using Excel the pre-programmed statistical function is NORMISINV.)

The process is:

1 use the version of the normal distribution tables in Appendix B to find z, then
2 use the conversion formula to find the mean.

1 Looking up 0.01 in Appendix B gives $z = 2.326$. However, Figure 8.19 indicates that as 100 g must be below the new mean, the value of z must be negative. Therefore $z = -2.326$.

2 The conversion formula is

$$z = \frac{x - \mu}{\sigma}$$

Putting all the known values into this conversion formula gives:

$$-2.326 = \frac{100 - \mu}{2.69}$$

i.e. $-2.326 \times 2.69 = 100 - \mu$
$-6.25694 = 100 - \mu$
$\mu = 100 + 6.25694$
$\mu = 106.25694$

If Mr Lee sets the machine to fill with a mean of 106.26 g he will meet the supermarket's requirement of fewer than 1 per cent of all jars containing under 100 g.

Case Study
Exercise 3

If the supermarket insisted that only 0.5 per cent of all jars contained fewer than 100 g, what should the new machine setting be changed to?

Case Study

Increasing the mean setting on the machine has meant that Ember Coffee supplies are using more coffee each week, with a resulting increase in costs. Mr Lee decides to seek advice from the manufacturer of the filling machine. The manufacturer suggests that he considers buying a new machine which is more consistent in filling the jars. It actually fills the jars with a reduced standard deviation. To cover the cost of the new machine Mr Lee needs to be able to reduce the mean setting to 101.5 g, and still achieve the super-market's target of only 1 per cent of jars containing fewer than 100 g (Figure 8.20). What is the largest value of the standard deviation, which ensures Mr. Lee meets these goals?

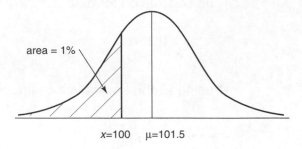

Figure 8.20 Normal distribution showing one per cent of jars containing fewer than 100 g and a mean of 101.5 g

Again, use the table in Appendix B to find the value of z which corresponds to an area in the tail of 0.01: $z = -2.326$. Then use the conversion formula:

$$z = \frac{x - \mu}{\sigma}$$

In this case we know everything except the standard deviation.

$$z = -2.326 = \frac{100 - 101.5}{\sigma}$$

$-2.326\sigma = 100 - 101.5$
$-2.326\sigma = -1.5$
$\sigma = 1.5/2.326 = 0.644884$

Mr Lee decides to order a new machine and asks the manufacturer to preset it to fill with a mean of 101.5 g and a standard deviation of 0.6 g.

Summary

In this chapter we looked at the **normal distribution**, which is a probability distribution occurring frequently in business situations. Typical examples of normal distributions can involve measurements, such as weight, length, volume etc. The normal distribution is a symmetrical distribution: the mean, median and mode coincide at the centre.

The chapter built on many of the statistical topics already covered. In particular probability, frequency/probability tables, means and standard deviations.

We looked at typical business situations where the data appeared to follow a normal distribution. Once we had established that the data did follow a normal distribution we were able to replace the actual distribution with the theoretical normal distribution and use normal distribution tables to establish the proportion of data falling into given ranges.

Further reading

Morris, C. (1996). Patterns of probability: Some distributions in *Quantitative Approaches in Business studies*, Pitman Publishing.
Probability distributions in *Quantitative Methods For First Year Degree Students*, BPP Publishing (1993).

1. Multiple choice
Circle the statement/s that you think is/are correct
1.1 All normal distributions have a mean of 0 and a standard deviation of 1
  (a) true
  (b) false
1.2 The shape of a normal distribution is:
  (a) skewed
  (b) symmetrical
  (c) cylindrical
  (d) bell shaped
1.3 For all normal distributions:
  (a) the mean = the mode
  (b) the mean = the median
  (c) the mean = the standard deviation
  (d) the mode = the standard deviation
1.4 Normal distribution tables give:
  (a) the value of the mean
  (b) the area under the curve
  (c) the height of the curve

2. Use the normal distribution tables to find the following probabilities:
(a) $p(z \geqslant 1)$
(b) $p(z \geqslant 2.05)$
(c) $p(z \geqslant -2.15)$
(d) $p(z \leqslant 1.3)$
(e) $p(1.3 \leqslant z \leqslant 1.6)$
(f) $p(-1.1 \leqslant z \leqslant 1.6)$
(g) $p(-1.3 \leqslant z \leqslant -0.6)$

3. Use the normal distribution tables to find the value of x for each of the following:
(a) $p(z \geqslant x) = 0.014$
(b) $p(z \geqslant x) = 0.18$
(c) $p(0 \leqslant z \leqslant x) = 0.47$
(d) $p(z \leqslant x) = 0.32$

4. A random variable follows a normal distribution with mean = 100 and standard deviation = 5, find the probability that:
(a) $p(x \geqslant 106)$
(b) $p(x \geqslant 110)$
(c) $p(x \leqslant 93)$
(d) $p(x \leqslant 97)$
(e) $p(95 \leqslant x \leqslant 102)$

5. The time of the first delivery of post at a city firm appears to follow a normal distribution, with a mean arrival time of 8.20 a.m. and with a standard deviation of 10 minutes. Estimate the number of times in the next 250 days that the post will arrive:
(a) before the receptionist arrives at 8 a.m.
(b) after 8.30 a.m. when the office staff start work
(c) during the daily meeting of heads of department, between 8.15 and 8.45 a.m.

6. A new type of battery is advertised as lasting for 45 hours of continuous use. In fact the life of these batteries follows a normal distribution with a mean of 46 hours and a standard deviation of 20 minutes. What percentage of batteries will not last for 45 hours of continuous use?

7. Case study
Clark's Electrical Supplies is a small family owned business producing accessories and spare parts for music systems. Mr Clark has

already identified a niche market for replacement packs of speaker leads, and successfully sells these wholesale. The leads are manufactured, then cut into lengths ready for packaging. The lengths of wire produced follow a normal distribution with a mean of 15 m and a standard deviation of 0.1 m.

Mr Hugo of Hugo Speakers Ltd, who is looking for a supplier of replacement wire for their new range of Hugo mini speakers, approaches Mr Clark. Hugo Speakers Ltd are proud of their high quality products and Mr Hugo insists that all suppliers meet his rigorous specifications. For the Hugo mini speakers, the length of the replacement wire must be between 14.95 and 15.10 m.

Mr Clark is so keen to supply the replacement wire that he tells Mr Hugo that he can meet the specification, and signs the contract, at a price of £15 per length. Using current production costs, Mr Clark considers that he will make a profit of £4 per length.

On returning to the factory Mr Clark tells his production manager about the new contract, but cannot understand why she is not as excited as he is. She is not sure whether she can meet the tight specification. She accepts that the current production cost is £11, but any lengths that are too short will need to be scrapped, at a cost of £12.50. She can recut any lengths that are too long, but this incurs an extra £5 per length.

She returns to her office and wonders what to do.

(a) What percentage of output meets Mr Hugo's specification?
(b) What is the expected cost of producing one acceptable length?
(c) What will be the expected profit per batch of 1000 lengths?

Chapter 9
Linear relationships in business

The aim of this chapter is to explore the nature of the relationship between two variables.

By the end of this chapter you will:

Aims

- recognize the importance of understanding the relationship between two variables
- know that exact mathematical relationships are unlikely to hold in most real-life situations
- be able to identify the independent and dependent variables from their descriptions
- be able to plot a scatter diagram and recognize when it suggests a relationship between two variables
- be aware of several different types of relationships that can exist between two variables
- be able to calculate the line of 'best fit' between two variables using the least squares method
- sensibly use the regression line for making realistic forecasts
- understand the concept of correlation between two variables
- be able to calculate and interpret the Pearson's product moment correlation coefficient
- be able to calculate and interpret Spearman's rank correlation coefficient.

- relationships between variables
- the difference between independent and dependent variables
- scatter diagrams
- linear relationships
- least squares regression
- analysis
- Pearson's product moment correlation coefficient
- Spearman's rank correlation coefficient
- correlation does not imply causation

Introduction

So far, our statistical analysis has been confined to just one variable. You now need to examine the relationships between two variables. Start by asking 'does a relationship exist?', 'what form does it take?', and 'how strong is it?' This is done by observing what is happening in the real world first and then trying to construct a mathematical model which reflects this. A mathematical model can be as straightforward as an equation linking two variables or as complex as the model used by the Meteorological Office to predict the weather, or the model used by the Treasury to predict the country's economy. All these models are trying to make theoretical predictions about a future happening. They have all had to be simplified in some form, and each model is based on a set of assumptions. Once a model has been constructed, it is then used to make predictions, which are, hopefully, reasonably accurate. The accuracy can eventually be checked against reality, and at this stage we may find that the model needs refining, or reformulating.

In this chapter we are going to construct two variable linear models by applying the techniques of **regression** and **correlation**. There are, of course, many different types of relationship, but this is the simplest form. It is encouraging to note that this basic approach underpins the more sophisticated relationships between variables.

Linear relationships between two variables

We looked at the mathematical form of the straight line in Chapter 1 and established that a straight line relationship can be expressed as:

$$y = a + bx$$

We also looked at drawing the graph of that relationship. It would be wise to re-read that section to refresh your memory.

Case Study

Every week the Budfordshire NHS Trust warehouse manager has to load used oxygen cylinders on to a supplier's lorry. He knows from past experience that it takes, on average, 4 minutes to back the lorry into the loading bay, open the tailgate, move the hoist into position and then close the tailgate on completion. This time does not vary with the number of empty oxygen cylinders he needs to load. It then takes about 3 minutes for each cylinder to be loaded.

Using this information he can estimate how long it will take each week to load the lorry. For example next week he has 10 cylinders to return, so he estimates this will take:

4 minutes + 10 × 3 minutes to load
= 4 + 30 minutes
= 34 minutes to load.

Case Study Exercise 1

What is the mathematical equation linking the number of cylinders and the time to load the lorry? Draw a graph of this relationship.

Would you be surprised if, next week, when there were 10 cylinders, the lorry actually took 36 minutes to load? Why?

In the Budfordshire NHS Trust case study it would have been surprising if it had taken exactly 34 minutes to load the lorry. After all, the 4 minutes and 3 minutes used in the calculation were averages. The 34 minutes calculated was a good guide.

In general we have to accept as a fact of life that deviations from the ideal model are caused by factors outside our control. These are usually referred to as **random errors**.

Case Study
Exercise 2

🖫

Can you identify any factors outside the control of the warehouse manager, which may cause the actual time taken to load the lorry to differ from the 34 minutes predicted?

In the case of Budfordshire NHS Trust the warehouse manager already knew the mathematical form of the relationship, but this is not always the case. Usually we have collected some data, a mass of figures which, on their own, do not convey much information and certainly do not give us any indication of the mathematical form of the relationship, or even, whether one exists.

We also need to establish which variable is *x* and which is *y*. The easiest way of determining which of your variables is *x* and which is *y* is to ask yourself: 'which variable depends on the other?' *y* is the dependent variable. In the case of the Budfordshire NHS Trust the time taken to load the lorry **depended** on the number of cylinders in the load, and the time taken is the *y* variable.

Remember

In general:

x is the independent variable and may explain changes in *y*, and *y* is the dependent variable and depends on *x*

Example

Mr Patel is the sales manager of a large agricultural feed merchants. He has a team of 10 sales representatives who travel the country, visiting farms, agricultural shows and taking orders for feed. He has noticed that there is a certain amount of variation in the level of orders the representatives achieve each month. He has decided to investigate this and has started by collecting some data. For each representative he has collected the number of farms in their area and the sales revenue achieved. The data collected is shown in Table 9.1. The sales revenue has been recorded as hundreds of pounds i.e. a recorded revenue of 1 represents sales of £100.

This data does not convey anything much at the moment.

Table 9.1 Number of farms and sales revenue

Number of farms in area	Sales revenue (£00s)
15	9
17	12
21	14
36	28
42	32
12	8
29	31
11	12
32	24
26	32

Of the two variables, the sales revenue should depend on the number of farms in the area. So the sales revenue will be *y* and the number of farms will be *x*.

The next step is to plot the data on a **scatter diagram** and have a look at its basic shape. The independent variable *x* goes on the horizontal axis and the dependent variable *y* on the vertical axis. We then plot the points on the graph, as shown in Figure 9.1, but we make no attempt to join them up. It is the underlying pattern we are looking at.

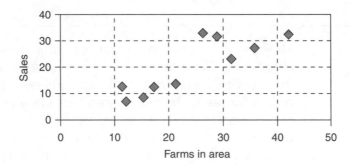

Figure 9.1 Scatter diagram showing the number of sales and the farms in the area

In this case, the points seem to cluster around a straight line. A larger number of farms seem to indicate a higher sales revenue.

There is, however, no indication of an exact mathematical relationship, but the pattern is sufficiently distinct to suggest that there may be a linear relationship between the two variables.

Some pairs of variables may indicate different patterns, or indeed, no discernible pattern. A selection of different types of scatter which might be observed is shown in Figure 9.2.

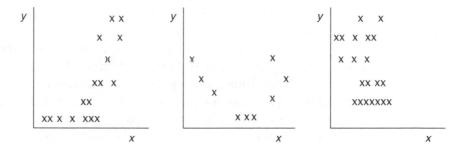

Figure 9.2 Scatter diagrams showing non-linear patterns in the area

It is always worth plotting a scatter diagram, as there is really no point in trying to fit a straight line relationship to any of the shapes shown in Figure 9.2.

Activity 1

A second-hand car dealer has been recording the age of the cars he is selling and the percentage the value has depreciated since they were new. The results are given in Table 9.2.

● Using this data plot a scatter diagram.
● Does there appear to be a relationship between the age of the car and the percentage depreciation?
● Can you think of any other factors which might affect the percentage depreciation?

Table 9.2 Age of cars and percentage depreciation

Age in years	0.5	1.0	1.1	2.0	2.4	2.5	2.8	3.2	4.0	4.5
Depreciation	33%	20%	45%	63%	55%	63%	65%	60%	88%	85%

Fitting the line

Once we are fairly certain that there is a straight-line relationship linking our two variables, we need to locate the line which best fits the data. Of course we could always try and fit the line by eye onto the scatter diagram. Try drawing the line that you think best fits the data on the scatter diagram in Figure 9.1.

In doing this you probably tried to draw the line so that it went through the middle of the scatter, as close as possible to all the points. This is a very subjective way of fitting the line, and different people would draw the line in different places. Thankfully there is a mathematical way of fitting the line and finding its equation, called **least squares regression**.

There is no need to worry about the mathematical derivation of the equation: it is sufficient to know that the line is in a position which minimizes the square of the distance of each point from that line, as some of the points are above the line and some below. Figure 9.3 shows just three points from a scatter diagram and their deviations from the regression line. Simply summing the deviations of the points from the line means that they would cancel each other out. So we need to square the deviations in exactly the same way as we did for the standard deviations in Chapter 6.

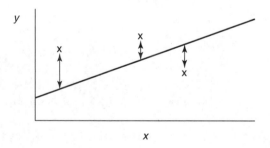

Figure 9.3 A portion of a scatter diagram with line showing three points and their deviations from the regression line

Calculating the least squares regression line

Earlier we recalled that a straight-line relationship can be expressed as:

$y = a + bx$

where:
- a = the intercept – i.e. the value of y when x is zero
- b = the slope of the line.

The data we have collected gives us pairs of values of x and y from which we need to calculate the values of a and b.

First calculate b using the formula:

$$b = \frac{\Sigma xy - n\bar{x}\,\bar{y}}{\Sigma x^2 - n\bar{x}^2}$$

where:

- Σxy is the sum of each x multiplied by its corresponding y
- n is the number of pairs of data
- $\bar{x}$ is the mean of x
- $\bar{y}$ is the mean of y
- Σx^2 is the sum of each x squared
- $\bar{x}^2$ is the mean of x, squared.

The calculation for a uses the value of b and the fact that the regression line always passes through the point $(\bar{x}, \bar{y})$.

$a = \bar{y} - b\bar{x}$

These calculations can be done quite easily using a spreadsheet.

Example

Let us return to Mr Patel and his sales representatives and calculate the regression line which fits his set of data. We have the number of farms as the independent (x) variable and the sales revenue as the dependent (y) variable. For ease of calculation put the data in a table, or set up a computer spreadsheet.

1 Calculate the values of xy by multiplying each value of x by its corresponding value of y: these figures go in the third column.
2 Square each value of x to give x^2 and put these values in the fourth column.
3 Add up the columns.
4 Then put the values calculated in the formula for b.

Table 9.3 Calculations to find the value of b

Number of farms x	Sales revenue y	xy	x^2
15	9	135	225
17	12	204	289
21	14	294	441
36	28	1008	1296
42	32	1344	1764
12	8	96	144
29	31	899	841
11	12	132	121
32	24	768	1024
26	32	832	676
Total $\Sigma x = 241$	$\Sigma y = 202$	$\Sigma xy = 5712$	$\Sigma x^2 = 6821$
Mean 24.1	20.2		

This is shown in Table 9.3, giving:

$$b = \frac{\Sigma xy - n\bar{x}\,\bar{y}}{\Sigma x^2 - nx^2}$$

$$b = \frac{(5712 - 10 \times 24.1 \times 20.2)}{(6821 - 10 \times 24.1 \times 24.1)}$$

$$b = \frac{(5712 - 4868.2)}{(6821 - 5808.1)}$$

$$b = \frac{843.8}{1012.9} = 0.833305$$

$b = 0.83$ to two decimal places

The slope of the line is 0.83.

This means that for every extra farm that a sales representative has in his/her area there will be, on average, 0.83 hundreds of pounds of extra sales. Remember that we had used hundreds of pounds of sales as our y variable. In other words every extra farm should result in £83 worth of extra sales.

To find the value of a, the intercept, put the values of $\bar{x}$, $\bar{y}$, and b into the formula:

$a = \bar{y} - b\bar{x}$

In this case:

$a = 20.2 - 0.833 \times 20.075$
$a = 20.2 - 20.075$
$a = 0.12$

Here the value of a is the sales revenue expected when a sales representative does not have any farms (i.e. when $x = 0$). Once again this is in hundreds of pounds, making the sales revenue £12 when a sales representative does not have any farms.

We might have expected this value to be zero since, if the sales representatives do not visit any farms they might not achieve any sales. They do, however, attend some agricultural shows so they may get a few sales there.

The equation representing the relationship between sales revenue, y (measured in hundreds of pounds) and the number of farms, x, is:

$y = 0.12 + 0.83x$

Case Study

The Budfordshire NHS Trust warehouse manager has found out that there is a new faster loading system available and decides to get one on approval. During this time, he plans to test the speed of loading and see if it really is faster than the old system. He arranges for the new system to be installed and for the next ten weeks, records the number of cylinders being loaded each day and times the loading. His test results are set out in Table 9.4.

Table 9.4 New loading times

Number of cylinders	Time taken
4	8
11	9
19	11
14	12
22	18
32	19
16	20
29	24
34	29
39	30

At the end of the ten weeks he has to decide whether the new system is really faster than the old. He starts by plotting the data on a scatter diagram (Figure 9.4) to see if the new relationship between time and cylinders is also linear.

Allowing for a certain amount of 'scatter' it appears that there is still an underlying straight-line relationship between the two variables. The warehouse manager decides to find the equation of this line using least squares regression. This will enable him to calculate the time to load just one cylinder and then he can compare the speed of the two systems. The data and the calculations are set out in Table 9.5. The calculations can be done using a spreadsheet.

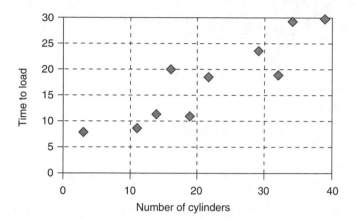

Figure 9.4 Scatter diagram showing the new time to load the cylinders

Table 9.5 Calculations to find the regression coefficients for the new loading system

| Number of cylinders | Time taken to load | | |
x	y	xy	x²
4	8	32	16
11	9	99	121
19	11	209	361
14	12	168	196
22	18	396	484
32	19	608	1024
16	20	320	256
29	24	696	841
34	29	986	1156
39	30	1170	1521
Total = $\Sigma x = 220$	$\Sigma y = 180$	$\Sigma xy = 4684$	$\Sigma x^2 = 5976$
Mean = 22	18		

As there were ten observations, $n = 10$

The formula for the slope of b, the slope of the line, is:

$$b = \frac{\Sigma xy - n\bar{x}\,\bar{y}}{\Sigma x^2 - n\bar{x}^2}$$

Putting the values just calculated into this formula gives:

$$b = \frac{4684 - 10 \times 22 \times 18}{5976 - 10 \times 22 \times 22}$$

$$b = \frac{4684 - 3960}{5976 - 4840}$$

$$b = \frac{724}{1136} = 0.637$$

or $b = 0.64$ to two decimal places.

The time to load one cylinder using the new system is 0.64 minutes. This is much faster than the old system, where, you will remember, the time to load one cylinder was 3 minutes.

The value of a, the intercept, is found by using the formula:

$$a = \bar{y} - b\bar{x}$$

Our new values give:

$a = 18 - 0.637 \times 22$
$a = 18 - 14.014$
$a = 3.986$
$a = 3.99$ minutes to two decimal places.

This is about the same as the old system. For the new system the equation linking loading time to the number of cylinders is:

$$y = 3.99 + 0.64x$$

Time to load = 3.99 + 0.64 × the number of cylinders to be loaded.

Overall the new system seems faster than the old, so the warehouse manager decides that he wants to purchase the new system.

The new regression equation will allow him to forecast how long he needs to allocate each week to the loading of the cylinders. Excel has the calculations for the slope and the intercept pre-programmed.

Activity 2

Return to Activity 1 earlier.
Here the second-hand car salesman was looking at the age of cars and the percentage depreciation in price.

- Calculate the least squares regression line that fits this set of data.
- What do you predict the percentage depreciation will be on a car that is 3.5 years old?

The correlation coefficient

Up to now we have looked at the scatter diagram and decided whether there appeared to be a straight-line relationship between the two variables, and then found the equation of the line. We have accepted that some degree of scatter can be tolerated on the assumption that there will always be a small random error. However, at some point we shall have to decide whether or not the scatter is sufficiently compact to make the assumption of a linear relationship credible. The regression equation does not tell us how close the line is to the data points on the scatter diagram. The line of 'best fit' is not necessarily a 'good fit'.

Figure 9.5 shows two scatter diagrams for two different sets of data, and their regression lines. Looking at the first, the data is very close to the line, indicating a good fit. The second set of data is widely spread around the line, and the regression line is not a good fit.

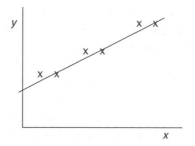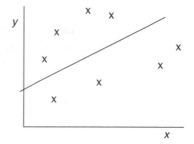

Figure 9.5 Scatter diagrams

Deciding by eye whether the line is a good fit is not really satisfactory, as different people will make different judgements.

The correlation coefficient, r for short, is a statistical measure of the strength of the relationship between the two variables. Its values lie between +1 and −1. The + or − sign indicates the direction of the relationship. The plus sign means that as x increases so does y: a positive correlation. A minus sign means that as x increases y decreases: a negative correlation. You should note that:

- A value of zero means that there is no correlation between the variables.
- A value of +1 means that there is perfect positive correlation: all the data points lie on the regression line.
- A value of −1 means that there is perfect negative correlation, again all the data points are on the line.

These are shown in Figure 9.6.

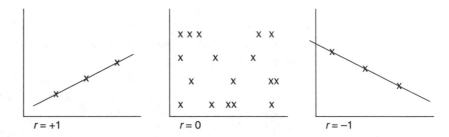

$r = +1$ $r = 0$ $r = -1$

Figure 9.6 Examples of perfect correlations and no correlation

In reality it is most unlikely that we would get +1, 0, or −1 as actual values of r. As we have seen so far, the points are usually spread around the line. It is the extent of that spread that we are interested in. As a rough guide, the numerical value of r should be at least 0.7, either positive or negative, before we can assume the existence of a relationship between two variables.

More usual examples of correlation are shown in Figure 9.7.

The full name of the measure used is Pearson's product moment correlation coefficient, named after the statistician who derived it.

The formula looks horrendous, but is not too difficult to calculate, particularly as we have already found most of the figures in the calculation of the slope of the regression line.

$$r = \frac{\sum xy - n\bar{x}\,\bar{y}}{\sqrt{(\sum x^2 - n\bar{x}^2)(\sum y^2 - n\bar{y}^2)}}$$

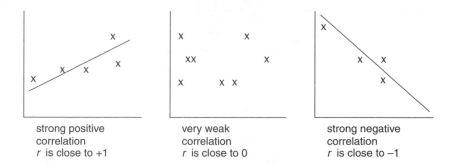

strong positive
correlation
r is close to +1

very weak
correlation
r is close to 0

strong negative
correlation
r is close to –1

Figure 9.7 Examples of different correlations

If you compare this with the calculations for *b*, the slope of the
regression line, you will see that, for a set of data, we have already
found the values of:

● $\Sigma xy - n\bar{x}\bar{y}$ (this is the numerator)
● $\bar{y}$ (this is the mean of *y*)
● $\Sigma x^2 - n\bar{x}^2$ (this is the denominator)

To find the correlation coefficient we need one extra column for y^2
on the table or spreadsheet. Summing this new column will give us
Σy^2.

Calculate the correlation coefficient for Mr Patel's sales representatives. Turn back to Table 9.3, the table of calculations to
find the values of the regression coefficients. The values needed for the correlation coefficient, extracted from that table, are:

● $\Sigma xy - n\bar{x}\bar{y}$ = 843.8
● $\bar{y}$ = 20.2
● $\Sigma x^2 - n\bar{x}^2$ = 1012.9

To complete the calculations add a y^2 column to the table, then
total it, as shown in Table 9.6.

$$r = \frac{843.8}{\sqrt{1012.9 \times (4998 - 10 \times 20.2 \times 20.2)}}$$

$$= \frac{843.8}{\sqrt{1012.9 \times (4998 - 4080.4)}}$$

$$= \frac{843.8}{\sqrt{1012.9 \times 917.6}}$$

$$= \frac{843.8}{\sqrt{929437.04}}$$

$$= \frac{843.8}{964.07}$$

$$= 0.88$$

Table 9.6 The calculations to find the value of the correlation coefficient between the number of farms and revenue

Number of farms x	Sales revenue y	xy	x^2	y^2
15	9	135	225	81
17	12	204	289	144
21	14	294	441	196
36	28	1008	1296	784
42	32	1344	1764	1024
12	8	96	144	64
29	31	899	841	961
11	12	132	121	144
32	24	768	1024	576
26	32	832	676	1024
Total = Σx = 241	Σy = 202	Σxy = 5712	Σx^2 = 6821	Σy^2 = 4998
Mean = 24.1	20.2			

The value of r at 0.88 shows that there is a positive correlation between the sales and the number of farms, and Mr Patel can be fairly confident about any forecast sales using the regression equation.

Case Study

Before purchasing the new loading system, the Budfordshire NHS Trust warehouse manager decides to calculate Pearson's product moment correlation coefficient for the data he has collected. He recognizes that just looking at the amount of scatter is not sufficiently rigorous, and as the new system is expensive, he really wants to be sure of his facts before presenting his results to the Trust's finance director. The calculations are shown in Table 9.7.

Table 9.7 Calculations to find the correlation coefficient for Budfordshire NHS Trust

| Number of cylinders | Time taken to load | | | |
x	y	xy	x^2	y^2
4	8	32	16	64
11	9	99	121	81
19	11	209	361	121
14	12	168	196	144
22	18	396	484	324
32	19	608	1024	361
16	20	320	256	400
29	24	696	841	576
34	29	986	1156	841
39	30	1170	1521	900
Total = Σx = 220	Σy = 180	Σxy = 4684	Σx^2 = 5976	Σy^2 = 3812
Mean = 22	18			

$$r = \frac{\Sigma xy - n\bar{x}\bar{y}}{\sqrt{(\Sigma x^2 - n\bar{x}^2)(\Sigma y^2 - n\bar{y}^2)}}$$

From our earlier calculations we know that

- $\Sigma xy - n\bar{x}\bar{y} = 724$
- $\bar{y} = 18$
- $\Sigma x^2 - n\bar{x}^2 = 1136$

Totalling the fourth column of the table gives:

- $\Sigma y^2 = 3812$

Putting these values into the formula for r gives:

$$r = \frac{724}{\sqrt{(1136) \times (3812 - 10 \times 18 \times 18)}}$$

$$= \frac{724}{\sqrt{1136 \times (3812 - 3240)}}$$

$$= \frac{724}{\sqrt{1136 \times 572}}$$

$$= \frac{724}{\sqrt{649792}}$$

$$= \frac{724}{806.1}$$

$$= 0.898$$

This indicates a reasonably strong correlation between the number of cylinders and the time taken to load them. As a result the warehouse manager feels fairly confident when he goes to meet the finance director.

Activity 3

Return to Activity 2 earlier. Calculate the value of Pearson's product moment correlation coefficient for the relationship between the age of the second-hand cars and the percentage depreciation.

Once again Excel has the calculations for the correlation coefficient pre-programmed.

A few words of caution

Correlation analysis is a useful and fairly easy technique to use, particularly as it is a pre-programmed function on most spreadsheets. Because of this it is often open to abuse.

The fact that x and y are correlated does not mean that x causes y, or vice versa. Correlation does **not** explain cause and effect – it is a mathematical process. You, the user, must decide whether or not it is reasonable in the first place to suggest a linear relationship. The correlation coefficient can only test whether the observed data supports the proposal.

It could even be that the scatter diagram shows that the relationship between the two variables is a curve. Here the correlation may be a very low figure, showing only that the relationship is not linear.

In some situations the two variables may each be related to an unknown, or undetected third variable. Often some economic factors produce a high correlation. However, these may just show that each factor is steadily increasing over time.

Rank correlation

Often in business and, particularly in market research, we are not able to measure actual quantities on a genuine scale. Instead we have, or can get, the individual items ranked in order of preference or ranked by size or by some other criteria. A typical example could be to ask two householders to rank ten different detergents in order of preference. The two variables are now the two sets of rankings given by the two householders. Each set of data is simply the numbers 1 to 10 – just in a different order. The issue now is are two sets of rankings correlated?

As before, we could calculate Pearson's product moment correlation coefficient. However, there is a much simpler version which applies only to rankings.

Spearman's rank correlation

Spearman, who worked for Pearson, derived his correlation from Pearson's, using the fact that two sets of rankings are the same numbers but positioned in a different order. We will not go through the derivation here, but the formula for Spearman's rank correlation is:

$$r_{\text{rank}} = 1 - \frac{6\Sigma d^2}{n(n^2 - 1)}$$

where:

- n = the number of pairs of rankings
- d = the difference between the ranks for each of the two variables.

Example

A market research agency asked two householders to use ten detergents, each for a week, and then rank them in order of preference. The results are given in Table 9.8. Is there any correlation between the two householders' rankings of the detergents?

Table 9.8 Householders' rankings of ten detergents

Detergent	First householder's rankings	Second householder's rankings
A	3	7
B	1	4
C	5	1
D	8	5
E	2	6
F	7	10
G	9	3
H	6	9
I	10	8
J	4	2

Here there are ten pairs of rankings; therefore $n = 10$. To calculate d, the difference in the rankings, for each detergent subtract the second householder's rankings from those of the first, as shown in Table 9.9.

- Σd^2 is the total of the d^2 column =128

(Note: the total of the d column should be zero.)

Putting the values into the formula:

$$r_{rank} = 1 - \frac{6\Sigma d^2}{n(n^2 - 1)}$$

$$= 1 - \frac{6 \times 128}{10 \times (10^2 - 1)}$$

$$= 1 - \frac{768}{10 \times 99} \quad = 1 - \frac{768}{990}$$

$$= 1 - 0.776$$
$$= 0.224$$

Table 9.9 Calculations to find the correlation coefficient for the householders' rankings of detergents

Detergent	First householder's rankings	Second householder's rankings	d	d^2
A	3	7	−4	16
B	1	4	−3	9
C	5	1	4	16
D	8	5	3	9
E	2	6	−4	16
F	7	10	−3	9
G	9	3	6	36
H	6	9	−3	9
I	10	8	2	4
J	4	2	2	4
			Total	= 128

Applying the same criteria as earlier for determining whether the value of r indicates a correlation, we would conclude that there is no correlation between the two sets of rankings given by the householders.

We should only use the rank correlation when we do not have access to measured data. The rank correlation is less accurate than Pearson's correlation coefficient, as it is only based on rankings. For instance we cannot tell whether the difference between first and second places is the same as the difference between second and third places. We must be even more cautious in our interpretation of rank correlations.

Activity 4

A panel of bar staff was asked to taste a selection of ten speciality beers and produce one ranking of the beers in order of overall preference. They ranked the beers as shown in Table 9.10.

Table 9.10 Ranking of beer

Beer	A	B	C	D	E	F	G	H	I	J
Ranking	4	2	6	8	1 (best)	3	10 (worst)	7	5	9

Is there any correlation between these rankings based on taste and the amount of hops used in producing the beers as shown in Table 9.11?

Table 9.11 Percentage hop content in the beers tasted

Beer	A	B	C	D	E	F	G	H	I	J
% hops	0.1	0.25	0.05	0.08	0.23	0.20	0.01	0.04	0.15	0.02

Note: you will have to convert the percentage of hops used into rankings. Rank the beer with the largest percentage of hops as 1, the beer with the next highest percentage hops as 2 etc.

Case Study

Each year the journal of the Institute of Management, *Management Today*, in conjunction with Loughborough Business School, survey Britain's ten largest public companies in 26 sectors to evaluate their peers. Participating companies voted for their favourite company, outside their own sector, in nine different performance categories. The performance categories range from quality of management to quality of services, value as a long-term investment, community and environmental responsibility, quality of goods/services etc. The results for 1996 and 1997 are given in Table 9.12.

Table 9.12 Cross-sector winners

1997	1996	Company
1	1	Marks and Spencer
2	2	Tesco
3	8	Virgin
4	5	BT
5	3	Glaxo Wellcome
6	7	BP
7	4	British Airways
8	9	Shell Transport and Trading
9	–	Unilever*
10	6	Reuters

*Unilever did not appear in the 'top ten' cross-sector winners in 1996. However, for our purpose we will allocate it a rank of 10.

Published by kind permission of Management Publications, The Institute of Management and Loughborough University Business School.

Marks and Spencer topped the poll in both years. In 1997 it was voted the favourite company in five of the nine categories. Tesco retained second place, and coming up fast is Virgin. Virgin was voted number one in two categories: capacity to innovate and quality of its marketing.

Case Study Exercise 3

- What is the value of Spearman's rank correlation for the two years' rankings?
- What does this tell us?
- Can you explain why this should be the case?

Summary

In this chapter we have looked at constructing a simple model based on two variables: an **independent** variable and a **dependent** variable. The data collected was plotted on a **scatter diagram** to get a visual first impression of any possible underlying pattern. If there seemed to be an underlying linear relationship then **regression analysis** enabled us to find the equation which best fits a set of data. These calculations are easily performed by most spreadsheet packages. This equation can then be used, with caution, to make **estimates or forecasts** of the dependent variable.

The **slope of the regression line (b)** is the change in the value of the dependent variable for a unit change in the independent variable.

The **intercept (a)** is the value of the dependent variable when the value of the independent variable is zero. Graphically, it is the point where the regression line crosses the y-axis.

The **correlation coefficient** measures, mathematically, the strength of the relationship between the two variables. It does not prove that one variable causes another to happen. It is even possible that the two variables are each related to an unknown third variable. Often unrelated economic variables appear correlated as they are both increasing over time. Sometimes we meet examples of spurious correlations. This can occur when two totally unconnected variables produce high correlation coefficients.

The correlation coefficient takes values between –1 and +1. The closer it is to 1 the better the positive correlation between the two variables. The closer to –1 the better the negative correlation. The closer to zero the poorer the correlation.

In this chapter we have only looked at two variables. However, in all the examples and the case studies, other variables were probably influencing the values of the dependent variable. Multiple regression takes account of these other possible independent variables. Multiple regression is based on the same foundation as simple linear regression, with the values of the intercept and slopes being interpreted in the same way. Obviously the calculations are more complex, but they are always done by computer.

Further reading

Morris, C. (1996). Looking for connections and spotting the relationship in *Quantitative Approaches in Business Studies.* Pitman Publishing.
Wisniewski, M. (1996). Business forecasting: simple linear regression in *Foundation Quantitative Methods for Business.* Pitman Publishing.

Self Assessment 1

1. Multiple choice
Circle the letter of the statement which you think corresponds to the correct answer.

1.1 The value of b in the regression equation:
(a) cannot be negative
(b) equals one when there is perfect correlation
(c) measures the increase in the y variable for unit increase in x
(d) measures the scatter of points around the regression line
(e) measures the value of the independent variable when the value of the dependent variable is zero

1.2 The value of a in the regression equation:
(a) cannot be negative
(b) measures the value of the independent variable
(c) is the value of the independent variable when the value of the dependent variable is zero
(d) is the value of the dependent variable when the value of the independent variable is zero
(e) must be positive

1.3 A correlation coefficient with a value of 0.9:
(a) indicates that x causes y
(b) indicates that y causes x
(c) indicates that the relationship between x and y is too strong to have been caused by chance
(d) shows that x and y have something in common

1.4 A regression line:
(a) shows the degree of correlation between two variables
(b) can be used to predict exact values of y for given values of x
(c) can be found by the method of least squares

1.5 A scatter diagram is used:
(a) to determine the pattern of the relationship between two variables
(b) to check the values found by the method of least squares regression
(c) to check the value of the correlation coefficient

2. Briefly explain the following:
2.1   A scatter diagram
2.2   The objectives of regression analysis
2.3   The dependent variable
2.4   The independent variable
2.5   The slope of the regression line
2.6   The y intercept
2.7   A positive correlation
2.8   A zero correlation
2.9   A rank correlation
2.10 Why one needs to be cautious when using regression and correlation

3. Problems to solve, using a calculator or a spreadsheet, such as Excel. Then check your answers using the pre-programmed function of the spreadsheet.
3.1 Table 9.13 shows the advertising expenditure and the sales turnover of a record shop during 1998:

Table 9.13 Advertising expenditure and sales of record shop

Month	Advertising expenditure (£'00)	Sales turnover (£'000)
Jan	24	341
Feb	21	314
Mar	18	301
Apr	14	294
May	16	306
June	19	310
July	28	364
Aug	34	387
Sep	24	347
Oct	18	306
Nov	26	349
Dec	32	402

(a) Plot a scatter diagram to determine the nature of the relationship
(b) If appropriate calculate:
   (i) the regression line which best fits the data
   (ii) the correlation coefficient

(iii) the predicted value of the sales in January 1999 when the advertising expenditure is planned to be £2900 and in February when the planned advertising expenditure is £2200.

3.2 A wool mill keeps the untreated fleeces in a storage area without the humidity being controlled. Over ten consecutive days the relative humidity in the storage area and the moisture content of a sample of fleeces were checked, both measurements are expressed as percentages. The results are shown in Table 9.14.

Table 9.14 Humidity and moisture content of fleeces

Humidity	Moisture content
46	10
30	7
34	9
52	13
38	8
44	12
40	9
45	10
31	8
60	14

Is there any correlation between the humidity level in the storage area and the moisture content of the fleeces?

3.3 During the first ten months of the year the demand for a product and the unit price are shown in Table 9.15.

(a) Using this information, calculate the demand function, i.e. the equation linking demand and price.
(b) What is the value of the correlation coefficient between demand and price?

3.4 Ten candidates are shortlisted for a new post in an accountancy firm. Each candidate completes an aptitude test and is then interviewed by the departmental manager. The test scores and the manager's order of preference for the candidates is given in Table 9.16.

Table 9.15 Product demand and unit price

Month	Demand ('000s)	Unit price (£)
Jan	18	20
Feb	19	19.50
Mar	22	18
Apr	15	21.50
May	18	19
Jun	19.5	20
July	16.5	21
Aug	17	20.5
Sept	20	19
Oct	20	19.5

Table 9.16 Aptitude test scores and manager's preference

Candidate	Aptitude test score	Manager's preference
A	16	3
B	12	7
C	10	6
D	8	8
E	19	5
F	10	4
G	17	1
H	11	9
I	13	10
J	15	2

Is there any correlation between the candidates' test scores and the manager's preference after their interviews?

4. Case studies

4.1 MUFTI Furniture is a large 'flat pack' furniture manufacturer supplying quality furniture to most department stores in the UK. The manager is concerned about the overhead costs in the final packaging section of the factory. For several years the manager has estimated the monthly overhead costs as being a fixed proportion of the direct labour costs. Recently his forecasts have been out by a considerable amount, so he has decided to rethink the relationship. He has checked his records for the past year and produced the set of data given in Table 9.17.

Table 9.17 MUFTI monthly records

Month	Direct labour(£) x	Overhead costs(£) y	Number of flat packs x	Cardboard metres x
Jan	3920	3100	1790	2400
Feb	3610	2650	1770	2160
Mar	3800	2970	1520	2240
Apr	3970	2750	3720	2190
May	3750	2810	5840	2210
June	3980	3040	4910	2350
July	3690	3220	6970	2510
Aug	3710	3160	6700	2450
Sept	3910	2960	3130	2260
Oct	3900	2540	6148	2130
Nov	3890	2830	1030	2280
Dec	3830	3060	4620	2380

Advise the manager on how he should forecast the overhead costs from now on.

4.2 Miss Smith is the inventory manager of a large components manufacturing company. Every component in the inventory has its own unique code which comprises both letters and numbers.

Miss Smith is concerned about the quality of information being input into her department's database by her team of input clerks. Each clerk enters details of customer orders received from the company's sales force. This information is vital and must be accurate to ensure that the correct components are sent to the customers.

Miss Smith has talked with her team and they have identified three possible reasons for the errors:

1 *Tiredness*: as the input process can be tedious it is possible that the clerks make more errors as the day goes by.
2 *The code*: as the unique code is made up of a mix of letters and numbers it is possible that the errors occur as the clerks change between numbers and letters on their keyboards.
3 *Noise from the factory*: often, when the factory is working to full capacity, the office is very noisy. This can be very distracting.

Miss Smith and her team then collect as much data as they can to help them get to the bottom of this problem. They record the percentage of error made at different times of the day, and with different levels of factory noise. Then they calculate the percentages of letter and numbers in the codes and the corresponding percentage of errors made.

Once the data is collected and tabulated, as in Table 9.18, they have decided to turn to you for help with the analysis and the determination of the underlying cause of the high percentage of errors.

Please advise Miss Smith and her team.

Table 9.18 Percentage of errors and possible causes

1. Tiredness		2. Code		3. Noise	
Time of day	% of errors	% letters	% of errors	Noise	% of errors
09.00	5.3	60	9.3	56	1.2
09.30	9.6	20	2.5	73	1.9
10.00	2.4	10	2.1	83	1.1
10.15	3.7	76	3.2	86	5.1
10.30	9.1	18	1.7	75	4.2
10.45	7.2	16	1.2	44	9.3
11.00	4.3	72	4.2	80	5.8
11.15	8.3	68	3.1	62	6.2
11.30	2.5	84	4.9	67	1.3
11.45	1.9	85	13.5	54	3.4
12.00	6.2	82	12.7	77	9.3
13.00	5.3	42	7.5	83	6.2
13.15	9.4	44	8.1	55	2.1
13.30	4.5	32	4.1	71	4.1
13.45	4.3	15	1.8	57	6.1
14.00	8.1	36	2.9	82	1.7
14.15	2.7	19	2.3	83	2.5
14.30	6.1	25	3.1	69	3.1
15.00	5.2	56	8.1	66	6.1
15.15	2.6	26	3.4	65	2.1
15.30	3.5	90	15.0	82	3.5
15.45	4.6	94	15.1	68	7.2
16.00	2.6	53	7.8	59	2.8
16.15	5.9	25	2.5	69	7.3
16.30	1.8	33	4.0		
16.45	2.2	15	2.1		
17.00	3.1	76	16.4		
17.15	5.6				
17.30	4.2				

Chapter 10

Fundamentals of business forecasting

By the end of this chapter you will be able to:

- understand the need for forecasting in business
- understand the differences between long-term and short-term forecasting
- use moving averages to calculate the underlying trend using historical data
- estimate seasonal variation from historical data
- make simple business forecasts using the underlying trend and seasonal variations.

- time series
- underlying trend
- moving averages
- seasonal variation

Introduction

This chapter is intended to introduce you to some useful forecasting techniques. In all businesses a perfect knowledge of the future would be a distinct advantage. We could plan production knowing the future demand for our products, know how many hospitals to build, or know when a machine will breakdown and need repairing. However, this is not possible. There is always uncertainty about the future, although the degree of uncertainty may vary. Forecasting techniques aim to reduce the level of uncertainty, and are based on past and present data. In most forecasting situations we are looking for patterns and trends, but there are always many factors causing irregularities around the underlying trend. For example Table 10.1 gives the quarterly sales of tee shirts sold by a market trader in each of the last four years. Exactly as we did in the chapter on regression and correlation, we can plot a scatter diagram and see if there are any obvious patterns. Time is the independent variable, and, in this case, sales of tee shirts is the dependent variable. This is shown in Figure 10.1. However, the scatter diagram seems to give little encouragement that there is any correlation between time and sales. However, each third quarter (the summer) is higher than the other three-quarters, and the first quarter (January to March) is always below the other quarters. There may be a gradual year-on-year increase in the sales. In this chapter we will try and find any underlying trends and seasonal variations and use these as a basis for forecasting future outcomes.

Table 10.1 Quarterly sales of tee shirts (£'00)

Year	Q1	Q2	Q3	Q4
1995	13	22	58	23
1996	16	28	61	25
1997	17	29	61	26
1998	18	30	65	29

All the forecasting techniques examined in this chapter relate to seeking underlying patterns and trends developing over time. These are called **time series analyses**.

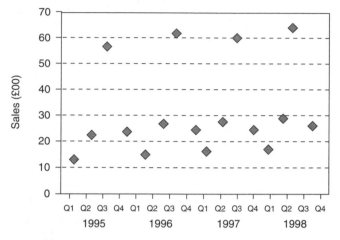

Figure 10.1 Sales of tee shirts

Long-term forecasting

Long-term forecasting is required for economic planning, some-times on a national scale, or for an organization's strategic business planning. The time span over which projections might have to be made can be ten years. In these situations sufficient past data covering many years is needed so that any underlying patterns can be seen. In Table 10.2, 19 consecutive years of past data, sales in this case, is available. Figure 10.2 is a scatter diagram for this data. Again,

Table 10.2 Sales for the past 19 years

Year	Sales (£000)	Year	Sales (£000)
1	100	11	138
2	179	12	218
3	201	13	297
4	188	14	237
5	150	15	187
6	126	16	161
7	197	17	240
8	282	18	325
9	215	19	258
10	168		

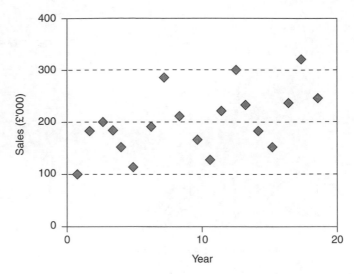

Figure 10.2 Scatter diagram of the last 19 years' sales

at this stage it is not easy to see any definite patterns. Joining the scatter points can help us see some of these, and this is done in Figure 10.3. There seem to be two main patterns: a long-term upward trend and a cyclical movement about this trend. These are shown in Figure 10.4. There are also fluctuations around these patterns, which could be seasonal and, as with regression, random variations.

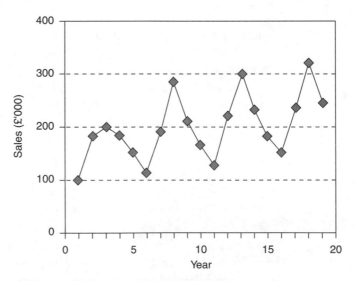

Figure 10.3 Line graph for last 19 years' sales

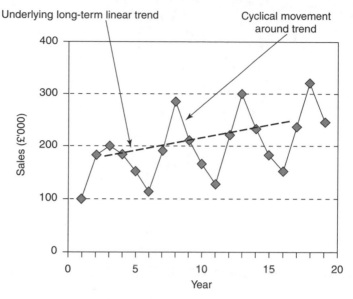

Figure 10.4 Line graph for last 19 years' sales showing the underlying trend and the cyclical variation around the trend

Long-term forecasting needs to take all these factors into account:

● Long-term trend
● Cyclical component
● Seasonal variation
● Random errors.

Adding the four components gives the simplest relationship between them – called the additive model:

Actual data = Trend component + Seasonal component + Cyclical component + Random component

There are many other models, including interactive models, where each component is related to all others.

Long-term forecasts are fraught with pitfalls and, in general, require very sophisticated forecasting techniques and computer simulation models.

Short-term forecasting

The data in Table 10.1 – the sales of tee shirts can be considered suitable for short-term forecasting. We have four years of data, and the

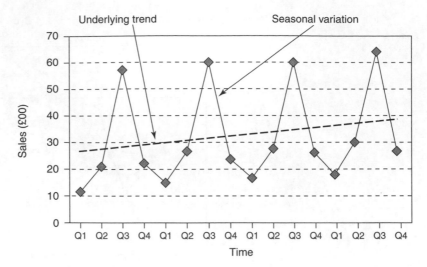

Figure 10.5 Quarterly sales of tee shirts with possible trend line superimposed

market trader probably only needs to forecast one year ahead. There appears to be a gradual yearly increase in sales and the data certainly exhibits seasonal variation. This is particularly marked in the third quarter of each year. Figure 10.5 is a line graph with a possible underlying upward trend superimposed on it. We can see that over a whole year the seasonal variation cancels itself out. The higher sales in the third quarter are balanced by lower sales in the others.

The short-term trend may be considered to coincide with a section of a longer-term cyclical component. The longer-term cyclical component can be downward, giving the impression of a downward short-term trend, within a long-term underlying upward trend. This can be seen in Figure 10.4 earlier.

In short-term forecasting, three components are usually considered:

● Short-term trend
● Seasonal component
● Random variation.

Again, the simplest model is the additive model:

Data = Trend component + Seasonal component + Random component

The short-term trend may be a section of a longer-term cyclical movement; there is no guarantee that it will continue upwards.

Estimating trend using moving averages

In all forecasting situations we need a method of finding the underlying trend. If the data, when plotted, appears to closely follow a straight line, then regression analysis is a suitable way of finding the equation of the line. However, there is a method called **moving averages** that will isolate the trend, whether or not it is linear. Moving averages 'smooth out' any regular seasonal or cyclical variation.

The sales data in Table 10.2 and shown as a line graph in Figure 10.3, appear to follow a five-year pattern. By averaging the data five years at a time, the variation around the trend line will be smoothed out. Taking the first five years' data and totalling gives:

The first **five-point moving total** = 100 + 179 + 201 + 188 + 150 = 818

Dividing by five gives the first **five-point moving average** = 818/5 = 163.6. This is the trend estimate of the middle of the five years used and so is the trend estimate for year 3.

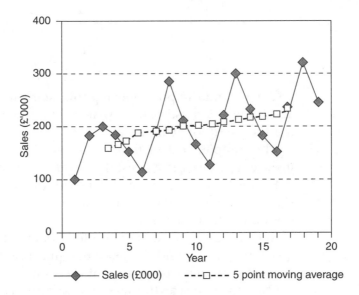

Figure 10.6 Sales data with five-point moving average superimposed

Table 10.3 Five-point moving average

Year	Sales (£000)	Five-point moving total	Five-point moving average
1	100		
2	179		
3	201	818	163.6
4	188	844	168.8
5	150	862	172.4
6	126	943	188.6
7	197	970	194
8	282	988	197.6
9	215	1000	200
10	168	1021	204.2
11	138	1036	207.2
12	218	1058	211.6
13	297	1077	215.4
14	237	1100	220
15	187	1122	224.4
16	161	1150	230
17	240	1171	234.2
18	325		
19	258		

The second five-point moving total starts with year 2, and the average is the trend estimate of year 4. The third starts with year 3, giving the trend for year 5.

The complete calculations are shown in Table 10.3, with the moving averages entered against the middle year of each five-year period.

Figure 10.6 shows the sales data with the five-point moving average superimposed. It shows that the moving average has effectively smoothed the time series.

Returning to the market trader's data. The data has a definite quarterly pattern and this seasonal quarterly variation is preventing us from getting a true picture of the trend.

Over a whole year the seasonal variation cancels itself out. Those quarters with sales above the trend will balance out those with sales below the trend. We can, therefore, take four quarters at a time and average them. This will effectively remove the seasonal variation, giving a sales value close to the trend line for the middle of the year.

As a first step towards averaging the first four quarters' data from Table 10.1 add their sales figures together. This gives:

13 + 22 + 58 + 23 = 116

Then, starting with quarter 2 of the first year, total the next four quarters giving:

22 + 58 + 23 + 16 = 119

Table 10.4 Four-point moving totals

Year	Quarter	Sales (£00)	Four-point moving total
1995	Q1	13	
	Q2	22	
			116
	Q3	58	
			119
	Q4	23	
			125
1996	Q1	16	
			128
	Q2	28	
			130
	Q3	61	
			131
	Q4	25	
			132
1997	Q1	17	
			132
	Q2	29	
			133
	Q3	61	
			134
	Q4	26	
			135
1998	Q1	18	
			139
	Q2	30	
			142
	Q3	65	
	Q4	29	

Again, this is a full year, even though it starts with quarter 2, and the seasonal variation should balance itself out.

These totals are called the four-point moving totals.

Continuing in this way produces the four-point moving totals shown in Table 10.4. On the time scale each total relates to the middle of the year. Again, this is shown on Table 10.4, where each total is entered in the middle of the year to which it applies. You will see that it no longer coincides with the original time scale. This will make it difficult for us to compare the actual sales with the four-point moving average sales (once we have divided each four point moving

Table 10.5 Eight-point moving totals

Year	Quarter	Sales (£00)	Four-point moving total	Eight-point moving total
1995	Q1	13		
	Q2	22		
			116	
	Q3	58		235
			119	
	Q4	23		244
			125	
1996	Q1	16		253
			128	
	Q2	28		258
			130	
	Q3	61		261
			131	
	Q4	25		263
			132	
1997	Q1	17		264
			132	
	Q2	29		265
			133	
	Q3	61		267
			134	
	Q4	26		269
			135	
1998	Q1	18		274
			139	
	Q2	30		281
			142	
	Q3	65		
	Q4	29		

Table 10.6 Estimates of trend based on eight-point moving averages

Year	Quarter	Sales (£00)	Four-point moving total	Eight-point moving total	Trend eight-point moving average
1995	Q1	13			
	Q2	22			
			116		
	Q3	58		235	29.375
			119		
	Q4	23		244	30.5
			125		
1996	Q1	16		253	31.625
			128		
	Q2	28		258	32.25
			130		
	Q3	61		261	32.625
			131		
	Q4	25		263	32.875
			132		
1997	Q1	17		264	33
			132		
	Q2	29		265	33.125
			133		
	Q3	61		267	33.375
			134		
	Q4	26		269	33.625
			135		
1998	Q1	18		274	34.25
			139		
	Q2	30		281	35.125
			142		
	Q3	65			
	Q4	29			

total by four). Happily there is a simple solution called centring the trend.

Take the four-point moving totals two at a time and total these, forming eight-point moving totals, as shown in Table 10.5.

Dividing each of these eight-point moving totals gives a **moving average** which is an estimate of the trend. This is shown in Table 10.6

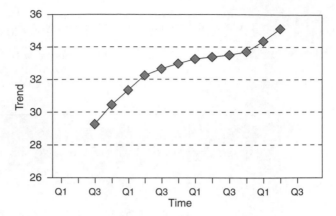

Figure 10.7 Estimates of trend

and the time scale coincides with the original time scale. These moving averages are shown graphically in Figure 10.7.

Figure 10.8 shows these moving averages superimposed on the original time series graph. It shows that the seasonal variations have been effectively smoothed out.

Estimating the seasonal variation

The method of the eight-point moving averages has given an estimate of the trend. We can use these figures to give an estimate of the seasonal variation. Figure 10.8 shows the relative positions of the

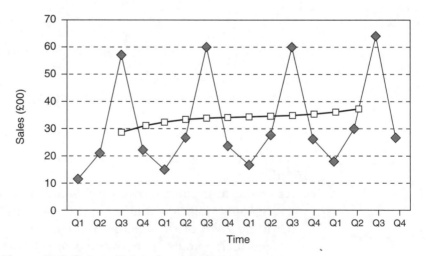

Figure 10.8 Sales with trend superimposed

trend and the actual data for each quarter. In our additive model, if we subtract the trend values from the actual data, we get the seasonal component plus the random component:

Sales − Trend component = Seasonal component + Random component

This is shown in Table 10.7, and summarized in Table 10.8. An average quarterly variation for each quarter has also been calculated, and

Table 10.7 Calculations to find deviation from trend

Quarter	Sales (£00)	Four-point moving total	Eight-point moving total	Trend	Deviation from trend (sales − trend)
Q1	13				
Q2	22				
		116			
Q3	58		235	29.375	28.625
		119			
Q4	23		244	30.5	−7.5
		125			
Q1	16		253	31.625	−15.625
		128			
Q2	28		258	32.25	−4.25
		130			
Q3	61		261	32.625	28.375
		131			
Q4	25		263	32.875	−7.875
		132			
Q1	17		264	33	−16
		132			
Q2	29		265	33.125	−4.125
		133			
Q3	61		267	33.375	27.625
		134			
Q4	26		269	33.625	−7.625
		135			
Q1	18		274	34.25	−16.25
		139			
Q2	30		281	35.125	−5.125
		142			
Q3	65				
Q4	29				

Table 10.8 Seasonal variation

Year	Quarter			
	Q1	Q2	Q3	Q4
1995			28.6	−7.5
1996	−15.6	−4.3	28.4	−7.9
1997	−16.0	−4.1	27.4	−7.6
1998	−16.3	−5.1		
Column total =	−47.9	−13.5	84.4	−23.0
Quarterly average =	−15.9	−4.5	28.1	−7.7

shown in the bottom row of this table. As expected the sales in quarter 3 each year are higher than the other quarters. On average they are 28.1 or £2810 (the data was in hundreds of pounds) above the underlying trend.

Over the course of a year the seasonal variation should balance out. We can check whether this is the case for an 'average year', which has average quarterly variation by totalling these figures:

−15.9
−4.5
+28.1
−7.7
Total = 0

Unfortunately, this is not always the case and sometimes minor adjustments need to be made to the quarterly variation to ensure they total to zero.

Forecasting

So far we have only analysed the historical data and we have not actually made a forecast. We have an estimate of the position of the trend and estimates of each quarter's variation from this trend. However, the market trader was interested in forecasting next year's sales. The forecast for each quarter of next year will be based on:

Forecast sales = Trend sales + Quarterly variation

Figure 10.7 illustrates that the trend, although upwards, it is not quite linear. The sales increase from 29.4 in the third quarter of 1995 to 35.1 in the second quarter of 1998. On average an increase of 0.475 each quarter. If this continues the trend component of the sales for:

- the third quarter of 1998 will be 35.1 + 0.475 = 35.575
- the fourth quarter of 1998 will be 35.1 + 2 × 0.475 = 36.05
- the first quarter of 1999 will be 35.1 + 3 × 0.475 = 36.525
- the second quarter of 1999 will be 35.1 + 4 × 0.475 = 37.0
- the third quarter of 1999 will be 35.1 + 5 × 0.475 = 37.475
- the fourth quarter of 1999 will be 35.1 + 6 × 0.475 = 37.95

Finally, each quarter's seasonal variation is added to the trend to give the forecast for the quarter:

- the first quarter of 1999 will be 36.525 − 15.9 = 20.625
- the second quarter of 1999 will be 37.0 − 4.5 = 32.5
- the third quarter of 1999 will be 37.475 + 28.1 = 65.575
- the fourth quarter of 1999 will be 37.95 − 7.7 = 30.25

The further ahead we forecast, the less reliable the figures will be. As mentioned earlier, the trend may change direction and decrease after several years of increasing. Or it may not increase at the same rate in the future.

Example

An independent financial advisor sells pensions to self-employed business people. Over the past four years, the sales of these pensions seem to fluctuate. In order for the advisor to plan his workload for next year, he is keen to find out whether there is any pattern in the sales. The quarterly sales for the past four years are shown in Table 10.9. These are plotted onto a scatter diagram, and this is shown in Figure 10.9. There appears to be a large amount of scatter. To see if the data follows any pattern, the data is then plotted as a line graph as shown in Figure 10.10.

There now appears to be a regular pattern across the quarters: the number of pensions sold in the first quarter of each year is higher than the other quarters, and the quarterly pattern is repeated each year.

Having established, from the graph, that there is a pattern of quarterly variation, with an underlying trend, we can use the method of moving averages to calculate the trend. This is shown in Table 10.10.

Table 10.9 Pensions sold by quarter

Year	Q1	Q2	Q3	Q4
1995	50	33	13	22
1996	55	36	15	28
1997	57	38	15	27
1998	60	38	17	29

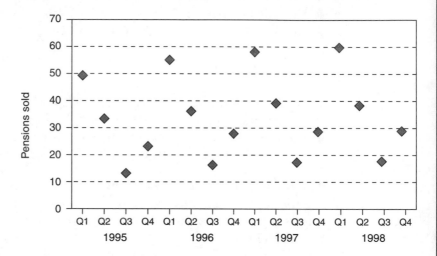

Figure 10.9 Scatter diagram of pensions sold by quarter

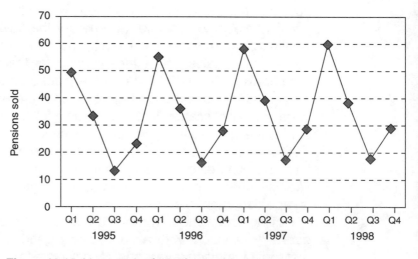

Figure 10.10 Line graph of pensions sold per quarter

Table 10.10 Calculations to find trend

Year	Quarter	Pensions sold	Four-point moving total	Eight-point moving total	Trend	Deviation from trend (pensions – trend)
1995	Q1	50				
	Q2	33				
			118			
	Q3	13		241	30.125	–17.125
			123			
	Q4	22		249	31.125	–9.125
			126			
1996	Q1	55		254	31.75	23.25
			128			
	Q2	36		262	32.75	3.25
			134			
	Q3	15		270	33.75	–18.75
			136			
	Q4	28		274	34.25	–6.25
			138			
1997	Q1	57		276	34.5	22.5
			138			
	Q2	38		275	34.375	3.625
			137			
	Q3	15		277	34.625	–19.625
			140			
	Q4	27		280	35	–8
			140			
1998	Q1	60		282	35.25	24.75
			142			
	Q2	38		286	35.75	2.25
			144			
	Q3	17				
	Q4	29				

Figure 10.11 shows the number of pensions sold with this trend superimposed. There is a gradual increasing trend from 30.125 in Q3 of 1995 to 35.75 in Q2 of 1998.

The quarterly variations calculated in Table 10.10 are transferred to Table 10.11, where the average variation for each quarter is found.

You will remember from earlier that in an 'average' year the

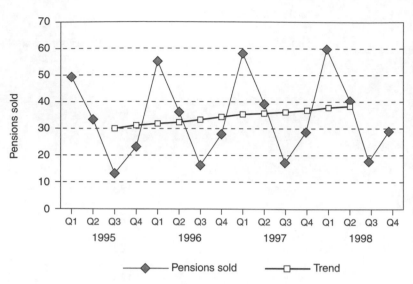

Figure 10.11 Pensions sold with trend superimposed

quarterly variation should balance out and total zero. This has not happened this time: the quarterly variations total 0.25. An adjustment of 0.0625 (0.25 divided by 4) needs to be subtracted from each quarterly variation, ensuring that the quarterly variation does balance out in the 'average' year.

The trend and the quarterly variation can be used to give forecasts of the number of pensions likely to be sold in 1999.

The trend increases from 30.125 in Q3 of 1995 to 35.75 in Q2 of 1998: an increase of 5.625 (35.75 − 30.125) across 12 quarters. This averages to an increase of 0.479 each quarter.

Forecasts There was insufficient data to enable us to calculate trend figures for Q3 and Q4 of 1998, and these will need to be forecast before we can make the 1999 forecasts. Firstly we shall need to forecast the underlying trend figures:

● 1998 Q3 = 35.75 + 0.479 = 36.229
● 1998 Q4 = 36.229 + 0.479 = 36.708
● 1999 Q1 = 36.708 +0.479 = 37.187
● 1999 Q2 = 37.187 + 0.479 = 37.66
● 1999 Q3 = 37.66 + 0.479 = 38.145
● 1999 Q4 = 38.145 + 0.479 = 38.624

Table 10.11 Calculations to find quarterly variation

Year	Q1	Q2	Q3	Q4	
1995			−17.125	−9.125	
1996	23.25	3.25	−18.75	−6.25	
1997	22.5	3.625	−19.625	−8	
1998	24.75	2.25			
Total =	70.5	9.125	−55.5	−23.375	
Average =	23.5	3.0417	−18.5	−7.7917	Total = 0.25
Adjustment	−0.0625	−0.0625	−0.0625	−0.0625	
Quarterly variation =	23.4375	2.9792	−18.5625	−7.8542	Total = 0
Quarterly variation (to 2 decimal places) =	23.44	2.98	−18.56	−7.85	Total = 0

Finally, to get the forecasts for 1999 add the quarterly variation giving:

- Forecast for Q1 = 37.187 + 23.44 = 60.627
- Forecast for Q2 = 37.66 + 2.98 = 40.64
- Forecast for Q3 = 38.145 − 18.56 = 19.585
- Forecast for Q4 = 38.624 − 7.85 = 30.774

Activity 1

Fastfreeze Foods supplies large packs of frozen chipped potatoes to the restaurant trade. Table 10.12 shows the number of packs (in thousands) supplied in the past five years.

1 Calculate the trend and seasonal components for this set of data.
2 How many packs will be required for each quarter next year?

Table 10.12 Packs of frozen chips supplied to the restaurant trade

Year	Quarter	Packs (000s)
1	Q1	48
	Q2	52
	Q3	16
	Q4	35
2	Q1	50
	Q2	46
	Q3	22
	Q4	40
3	Q1	68
	Q2	34
	Q3	26
	Q4	35
4	Q1	93
	Q2	56
	Q3	16
	Q4	45
5	Q1	84
	Q2	61
	Q3	29
	Q4	48

Other forecasting models

We have concentrated on the additive model, where the seasonal component is a fixed amount for each quarter and added to the underlying trend. Sometimes the seasonal variation can also vary with the trend. As the trend increases, or decreases, so does the seasonal variation. This is illustrated in Figure 10.12. Here the quarterly variations are percentages of the trend and the model is called a **multiplicative model**.

Data = Trend component × Seasonal component × Random component

The underlying trend is still found by moving averages.

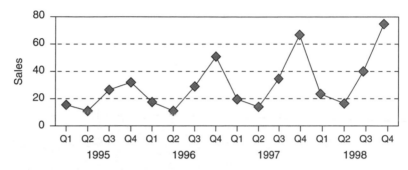

Figure 10.12 An illustration of a multiplicative model

This chapter intended to introduce you to some useful business forecasting techniques. Forecasting is a very wide topic, and we have only just scratched the surface. Some businesses use very complex computer-based forecasting models to plan their production, future investment and personnel requirements.

We considered the **additive model** for both **long- and short-term forecasting**, and incorporated the idea of **seasonal variation**.

Further reading

Forecasting can become very mathematical, and the specialized texts in this field cover the mathematics in great detail. Two suitable texts are:

Morris, C. (1996). More about forecasting in *Quantitative Approaches in Business Studies*. Pitman Publishing.

Wisniewski, M.(1994). Forecasting 1 in *Quantitative Methods for Decision Makers*. Pitman Publishing.

1. Forecasting
1.1 Why is forecasting useful for businesses?
1.2 What are the main components of:
   (a) a long-term forecast?
   (b) a short-term forecast?

2. Sales
2.1 Over the last 12 weeks a garage has sold the quantities of unleaded petrol shown in Table 10.13.

Table 10.13 Petrol sales

Week	Thousands of litres
1	170
2	250
3	190
4	210
5	280
6	200
7	220
8	290
9	220
10	240
11	300
12	220

(a) Plot the sales figures on a time series graph
(b) What type of pattern does the data appear to follow?
(c) Use the method of moving averages to estimate the trend
(d) Plot the trend that you have found on the time series graph

Table 10.14 Number of PCs sold

Year	Quarter	Sales ('000s)	Year	Quarter	Sales ('000s)
1	Q1	4.8	3	Q1	6
	Q2	4.1		Q2	5.6
	Q3	6		Q3	7.5
	Q4	6.5		Q4	7.8
2	Q1	5.8	4	Q1	6.3
	Q2	5.2		Q2	5.9
	Q3	6.8		Q3	8
	Q4	7.4		Q4	8.4

2.2 The number of PCs sold by an independent retailer each quarter for the past four years is shown in Table 10.14.
   (a) Plot the data on a time series graph
   (b) Calculate the trend using the method of moving averages
   (c) Calculate the quarterly variation
   (d) Forecast the sales for each quarter of next year

3. Case Study

Quickrepair is a family business specializing in repairing domestic appliances. For planning purposes the manager would like to forecast the number of washing machine repairs expected next year. He has available the number of repairs carried out each month for the past four years. This is shown in Table 10.15.

   The manager's daughter suggests that, as a first step, they plot the data on a graph to see if there is any obvious pattern. Then, if there is, try and use this to forecast the repairs for next year.

(a) Plot the data and determine the underlying pattern
(b) Use this as a basis for time series analysis
(c) Forecast the number of repairs expected next year

Table 10.15 Number of washing machine repairs carried out

Year	Month	Number of machines	Year	Month	Number of machines
1	Jan	111	3	Jan	136
	Feb	114		Feb	140
	Mar	117		Mar	134
	Apr	176		Apr	187
	May	165		May	183
	June	188		June	192
	July	203		July	223
	Aug	211		Aug	226
	Sept	197		Sept	222
	Oct	155		Oct	176
	Nov	156		Nov	168
	Dec	156		Dec	185
2	Jan	130	4	Jan	143
	Feb	135		Feb	140
	Mar	125		Mar	146
	Apr	181		Apr	189
	May	184		May	193
	June	179		June	186
	July	206		July	227
	Aug	211		Aug	226
	Sept	202		Sept	230
	Oct	162		Oct	180
	Nov	159		Nov	176
	Dec	164		Dec	186

Integrating case studies

Case Study 1

Select the annual report of a multinational company (these are usually available in large libraries). From this report find the company's turnover and profit for the last five reported years.

Then, by using the RPI for each of these years, deflate these figures to determine the company's performance after inflation has been taken into account. Possible sources of the RPI include the *Annual Abstract of Statistics*, other government publications, or from the Internet.

Write a short alternative company report based on your findings.

Case Study 2

At 9.55 a.m. on Tuesday 8 December Mrs Wang and her son Lee arrived at their doctor's surgery for Lee's 10 a.m. appointment. This is a group practice with up to four doctors available to see patients.

The Wangs were told by the receptionist to take a seat and wait. They would be called as soon as a doctor was free to see them. At 10.30 Mrs Wang asked the receptionist if they had been forgotten. No they hadn't, but surgery was running late, was the reply.

Lee Wang was eventually called to see a doctor at 10.45, his examination took 15 minutes and they left at 11 a.m.

As the surgery frequently runs late the receptionist decides to document the delays and present the evidence with her recommendations for improvement to the doctors at their next management meeting. She decides to make a verbal presentation covering the main points of her investigation using charts and diagrams as illustrations. She will also give each doctor a copy of her detailed written report to read later.

Suggest ways that the receptionist could collect the data she needs. The data actually collected is shown in Table CS2.1.

Table CS2.1 Data collected by the doctors' receptionist
Wednesday 14 May

Patient number	Appointment time	Arrival time	Called time	Departure time
1	8.30	8.20	8.35	8.45
2	8.30	8.25	8.40	8.50
3	8.40	8.30	8.55	0.00
4	8.40	8.45	8.55	9.15
5	8.45	8.30	8.55	9.10
6	8.45	8.35	9.05	9.20
7	9.00	8.55	9.10	9.30
8	9.00	8.50	9.15	9.30
9	9.00	8.55	9.20	9.35
10	9.00	8.55	9.15	9.20
11	9.00	8.55	9.20	9.30
12	9.00	9.00	9.30	9.40
13	9.10	9.00	9.40	9.50
14	9.10	9.05	9.45	10.00
15	9.10	9.00	9.55	10.00
16	9.10	9.15	9.50	10.05
17	9.15	9.10	10.00	10.10
18	9.25	9.15	10.05	10.15
19	9.30	9.20	10.00	10.10
20	9.30	9.25	10.10	10.20
21	9.40	9.30	10.20	10.30
22	9.45	9.35	10.30	10.40
23	9.50	9.45	10.30	10.45
24	9.55	9.50	10.40	10.50
25	10.00	10.05	10.50	11.00

On Wednesday 14 May three doctors arrived on time to start their surgery and one was late.

1 Analyse the data.

2 Make recommendations for improving the appointment system and service to the patients.
3 Prepare notes and diagrams for the receptionist to use when she makes her verbal report to the meeting.
4 Write a report to be given to the doctors.

Case Study 3

A car manufacturer buys 10 mm bolts from a local supplier. Bolts smaller than 9.95 mm will fall through the predrilled holes in the metal chassis.

Recently the fitters have noticed that more bolts than usual are too small, the supplier claims that because of the inherent variation in

Table CS3.1 Diameters of 200 bolts

9.96084	10.07257	10.00896	9.98861	9.98801	9.99664	9.99310	10.02904
9.94386	9.97336	9.98426	10.03423	9.98738	10.00242	10.01365	10.03628
10.00902	9.95257	10.01746	9.92562	10.02624	10.03508	9.95717	9.96344
9.89085	9.94090	10.00408	10.02663	10.00883	10.04086	9.93805	10.02399
9.98472	10.05555	9.96318	9.93828	9.96919	10.04976	9.97474	9.93337
9.94999	9.93210	10.06626	9.97174	10.00275	10.00689	9.98586	9.93732
10.00126	9.99381	9.99553	9.99960	9.94789	10.04171	9.92905	9.95285
10.05113	10.02843	10.02142	9.92445	9.98678	9.99927	9.97477	9.92661
9.93743	10.02320	9.91068	9.91722	9.96483	10.01168	9.91222	10.08033
9.95121	9.94873	9.98362	9.92853	10.02923	9.94263	9.97434	9.94206
10.06240	9.98734	9.99665	9.98429	10.08603	9.95595	10.06756	9.99594
9.93463	9.98467	9.96643	9.95656	9.94688	10.01942	10.05494	9.98768
9.90470	10.04437	10.01434	10.02955	10.00734	10.03335	9.93647	9.96889
9.97531	9.96044	9.98591	10.03006	9.95896	10.06176	9.94015	10.00448
9.97974	9.89837	10.09204	10.00439	9.99105	10.00283	9.97038	9.93498
9.94540	9.97375	10.02058	10.00744	9.96545	10.04409	10.00858	9.94946
10.01181	9.95823	9.92250	9.96471	9.95323	9.95344	10.04044	10.02439
9.93659	10.02973	9.99357	9.93459	9.94350	10.00657	10.07382	9.98480
10.02525	9.96111	9.96255	9.97828	9.93438	10.03425	10.04985	9.94225
10.05722	10.01654	10.03861	10.07091	10.04612	9.96929	10.01023	9.94177
9.97682	9.92872	9.95633	10.03393	9.98957	9.97649	9.97611	9.96103
10.02696	9.96095	9.97766	9.95876	9.96774	10.05694	10.00172	10.01249
9.94660	10.03088	9.99191	10.00008	9.98853	10.00333	9.95702	9.99020
9.97290	10.00790	9.98991	9.95764	9.96271	9.98680	9.99108	9.94311
9.97320	9.99745	9.99645	9.97579	9.95149	9.97295	9.99607	9.98367

the production process, the occasional bolt will be too small. The production process used produces bolts with a mean diameter of 10.01 mm and a standard deviation of 0.02 mm, the diameters appear to follow a normal distribution.

1 If the supplier is right, and the variation is solely due to the inherent variation in the production process, calculate the proportion of bolts that will be too small.
2 The fitters remain unconvinced and decide to accurately measure a sample of 200 bolts selected at random. Their diameters are given in Table CS3.1. Analyse the data for the fitters, and write a response to the supplier.

Case Study 4

Tim runs a small independent off-licence called 'Cheers and Things'. As Tim cannot afford to keep a large quantity of stock he needs to plan his weekly visits to the cash and carry carefully. He has a feeling that some of his sales may depend on the weather, if the weather is good his customers seem to buy more, they also appear to buy more during the public holidays, particularly over Christmas and the New Year.

To test this feeling he looks at last year's sales of wine, and requests a print out of the mean weekly daytime temperature, from the local meteorological office. The data is shown in Table CS4.1. Last year the dates of the public holidays were:

Good Friday   10 April
Easter Monday   13 April
Spring Bank Holiday   4 June
August Bank Holiday   31 August

Analyse this data for Tim, and produce a predictive model that will enable him to plan his weekly purchases from the cash and carry.

Table CS4.1 Wine sales and temperature

Week ending	Temperature degrees C	Bottles of house red wine	Bottles of house of white wine
04 Apr	10	213	438
11 Apr	12	188	606
18 Apr	13	200	575
25 Apr	13	275	469
02 May	11	238	500
09 May	12	213	469
16 May	14	213	531
23 May	17	288	563
30 May	19	213	625
06 Jun	20	225	594
13 Jun	21	200	750
20 Jun	19	275	563
27 Jun	18	250	625
04 Jul	20	300	563
11 Jul	18	263	563
18 Jul	25	263	688
25 Jul	24	225	656
01 Aug	26	263	719
08 Aug	23	200	688
15 Aug	17	188	594
22 Aug	16	213	563
29 Aug	15	200	594
05 Sep	17	188	656
12 Sep	15	288	563
19 Sep	19	263	594
26 Sep	20	200	594
03 Oct	17	188	500
10 Oct	15	250	500
17 Oct	12	200	500
24 Oct	11	250	438
31 Oct	13	250	500
07 Nov	10	300	469
14 Nov	9	250	438
21 Nov	9	213	406
28 Nov	7	238	375
05 Dec	4	238	375
12 Dec	6	213	406
19 Dec	3	250	344

(continued)

Week ending	Temperature degrees C	Bottles of house red wine	Bottles of house of white wine
26 Dec	3	275	594
02 Jan	1	238	594
09 Jan	2	238	325
16 Jan	0	300	313
23 Jan	−2	188	281
30 Jan	1	238	375
06 Feb	−3	238	281
13 Feb	4	300	406
20 Feb	3	188	375
27 Feb	2	238	344
06 Mar	5	200	375
13 Mar	7	188	469
20 Mar	8	225	500
27 Mar	6	225	531

Short answers

Chapter 1

Self-assessment 1.1

1 14
2 −80
3 −168
4 −8
5 −20

Self-assessment 1.2

1 −9
2 −25
3 4
4 −7
5 30

Self-assessment 1.3

1 0.8
2 1.1
3 0.006
4 2.5
5 0.3564
6 −31

Self-assessment 1.4

1 1.53
2 8.32
3 0.06
4 2
5 −26
6 −210

Self-assessment 1.5

1 2.57
2 3.456
3 89.4
4 2847
5 3800
6 194 000

Self-assessment 1.6

1 22.16
2 0.02
3 8.4
4 1 853 000
5 194 000
6 690 000

Self-assessment 1.7

1 3.125
2 3.333
3 6.667
4 5
5 156.25
6 270
7 £2.20
8 £70.50
9 0.5
10 0.333
11 0.0333

Self-assessment 1.8

1 7.143
2 6.667
3 11.111
4 55
5 15.625
6 85
7 £22.50
8 £91.65
9 0.5
10 0.147059
11 0.04

Self-assessment 1.9

1 10 000
2 0.01
3 8
4 4
5 10
6 2

Self-assessment 1.10

1 1000
2 0.1
3 64
4 4
5 100
6 2

Self-assessment 1.11

Any of the following:
$T = G - 100 - 20\%(G - 100)$
$T = G - 100 - 0.2(G - 100)$
$T = G - 100 - 0.2G + 20$
$T = 0.8G - 80$

Self-assessment 1.12

1 Unknowns:
Number of oranges = x
Number of cucumbers = y
Price of 500 g mince = p
Total cost = T
Return bus fare = $2 \times 5 \times 10$
$T = 2 \times 5 \times 10 + 15x + 50y + p$
$T = 100 + 15x + 50y + p$

2 Unknowns:
Cost per g of flour = f
Cost per g of yeast = y
Cost per ml of water = w
Total cost = C
$C = 3 + 55f + 2y + 300w$

Self-assessment 1.13

1 See Figure SA1

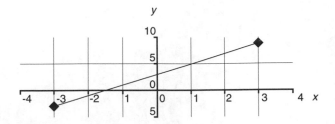

Figure SA1 Graph of $y = 3 + 2x$ from $x = -3$ to $x = +3$

2 See Figure SA2

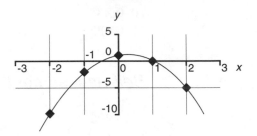

Figure SA2 Graph of $y = 1 + x - 2x^2$

Self-assessment 1.14

1 See Figure SA3

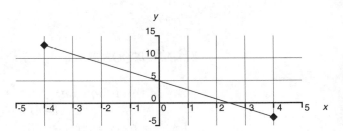

Figure SA3 Graph of $y = 5 - 2x$

2 See Figure SA4

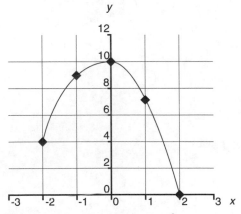

Figure SA4 Graph of $y = 10 - x - 2x^2$

Self-assessment 1.15

1   See Figure SA5

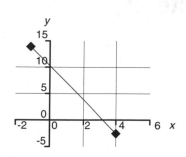

Figure SA5 Graph of $y = 10 - 3x$

2 See Figure SA6

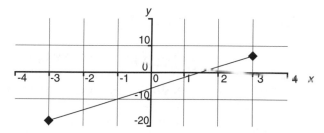

3 5
4 −3
5 by 10

Figure SA6 Graph of $y = -5 + 4x$

Self-assessment 1.16

1   See Figure SA7

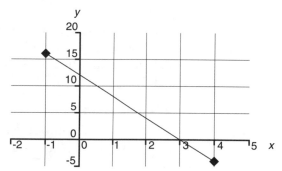

Figure SA7 Graph of $y = 12 - 4x$

2 See Figure SA8

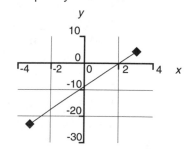

3 15
4 −23
5 by 5

Figure SA8 Graph of $y = -10 + 5x$

Chapter 2

Case study exercise 1: £35 714.29
Case study exercise 2: £34 029.81
Activity 1: Choose 'Package 2'
Activity 2: The investment is worth while
Activity 3: The second machine
Case study exercise 3: Option 2
Activity 4: 93.28
Activity 5: 92.17

Case study exercise 4

Pre-tax profits at 1994 prices

Year	1994	1995	1996	1997	1998
Profit	112 000	123 707.58	121 734.77	118 939.70	129 557.80

Self-assessment

1. Multiple choice
1.1) a; 1.2) b; 1.3) c; 1.4) b; 1.5) b; 1.6) a; 1.7) b

2. Progressions
2.1 The investment will be £307 72.
2.2 The investment will need to be £317 53.
2.3 Depreciate by £35 each year.
2.4 The PV is £587 73.

3. Index numbers
3.1 The index number = 133.33
3.2 (a) Laspeyre price index = 113.79; (b) Paasche price index = 114.02

4. Exercises
4.1 Depreciate by £880 each year.
4.2 The book value will be £11 616.
4.3 Investment A is better than investment B.
4.4 Choose Manufacturer 1.

5. Case study
Plan 3 gives the largest return, after tax, so Bob should choose this one.

Chapter 3

In most of the activities and exercises there is no one right answer.

Case Study Exercise 1

Speciality breads such as wholemeal, granary, French sticks, rolls, cakes, part-baked breads, sandwiches and pies.

Case Study Exercise 2

Discrete: the number of loaves to be baked each day, the number of staff required.
Continuous: the weights of the loaves
The flour, which Tudor needs, will be a discrete variable, if he buys it in sacks, or continuous if bought in bulk by weight.

Case Study Exercise 3

Tudor needs to collect primary data relating to the potential demand for his products, the prices customers are prepared to pay, the costs of making the new products (machinery, equipment, staff, insurance).

Case Study Exercise 4

The information needed can be found from government publications, company reports, and from the Internet.

Activity 1

Problems

There are a number of separate strategic problems such as:
1 Does Mr Williams want to:
   – maintain the membership when and if the new leisure centre opens
   – increase the membership

- encourage existing customers to visit more often
- encourage existing customers to spend more on each visit

2 Why and in what direction does Mr. Williams need to diversify by adding extra facilities?
3 What will be the effect of increased competition?

There are also a number of operational problems, such as:

1 Is the lack of a car park a problem for the customers?
2 Will the provision of a car park increase the use of the centre or just be used by other visitors to the town?
3 Do the current customers want any of the extra facilities being considered?
4 Would the new facilities attract any new customers?
5 What will be the economic and legislative implications of the new facilities?

Information

The answers to some of the questions raised may well be available.

1 Desk research using secondary data will give Mr Williams an indication of population and economic trends in the town, an idea of the costs of extra staff, any new health and safety regulations that will apply.
2 A survey of existing customers will give the answers to some of the questions.
3 A survey of potential customers may give the answers to other questions (of course it will be difficult to identify potential customers).

Case Study Exercise 5

A quota sample is probably suitable here. The quota is determined by the composition of the town's population.

Activity 2

You could observe the branch at different times of the day, on different days of the week. You could observe the:

- cleanliness of the branch
- the length of the queue
- the time customers queue
- how long the queue has to be before another service point opens
- whether the branch has wheelchair access
- whether there are special facilities for the old or infirm

You could also be a 'mystery customer' and observe:

- the way staff deal with customers
- the quality of service
- the helpfulness of the staff
- the way staff deal with customer difficulties

Activity 3

The idea here is to design a simple questionnaire asking existing users if they would use the new facilities and if so how often. Are they likely to use the centre more frequently if these facilities were available? Which of the new facilities is the most popular?

Self-assessment

1. Variables
(a) continuous; (b) discrete; (c) discrete; (d) discrete; (e) usually considered to be continuous

2. Samples
2.1 Information gathered from a sample is usually taken as being representative of the population.
2.2 No. A trailer is designed to encourage people to visit the cinema to see the whole film. It uses the most exciting and interesting parts of the film.
2.3 Sampling process
(a) Each of the three groups of employees needs to be sampled. Each sample should be stratified by gender and age group. The sampling frames will be the lists of employees in each job role.
(b) Either simple random sampling or stratified sampling.
(c) To elicit the views of existing customers: survey all the customers in the pub at specific times – cluster sampling. Determining the views of potential customers is more difficult, but the publican

could use a quota sample of people in the catchment area.

3. Data collection
(a) and (b) can be found in the *Annual Abstract of Statistics*
(c) and (d) can be found in *Social Trends*

4. Ideas for the case study
The secondary data can be found from a variety of sources such as the Internet and government publications.

The primary data can be found by surveying current medical students, GPs, hospital consultants (i.e. doctors who chose not to become GPs). A sample is needed for each population and each requires its own set of questions.

Chapter 4

Self-assessment

1. Short questions
1.1 (a) A bar chart – a popular way of presenting data. Can be used in a number of forms: simple, multiple, component and percentage component.
  (b) A pie diagram – another popular way of presenting data. Useful as a way of showing how a variable is split into its component parts.
  (c) Occasionally data may be misrepresented by cunning use of the vertical scale, or even omitting it altogether.
1.2 A properly constructed table can help the reader to understand a set of data better, and can assist the reader in making comparisons between two different subsets of the variables.
1.3 Good, clear diagrams assist the reader or audience in understanding the important features of a set of data. Many people are put off by numbers and tables of data.
1.4 Percentages are useful in a table when the sets of data to be compared are different sizes.
1.5 They must all have a title, row and column headings, the source of data referenced, and a key.

Chapter 5

Activity 1

Largest number = 277
Smallest number = 211

Weekly wage x	Frequency f
211 to 220	11
221 to 230	20
231 to 240	25
241 to 250	14
251 to 260	7
261 to 270	5
271 to 280	2
Total =	84

Activity 2

Maximum value = 6.93
Minimum value = 0.7

Frequency table showing the new response rates:

Response rate in mins (x)	Frequency
$0 < x \leqslant 1$	4
$1 < x \leqslant 2$	14
$2 < x \leqslant 3$	19
$3 < x \leqslant 4$	11
$4 < x \leqslant 5$	6
$5 < x \leqslant 6$	4
$6 < x \leqslant 7$	2
Total =	60

Cumulative frequency table showing the new response rates

Response time	Cumulative frequency
	0
1 and under	4
2 and under	18
3 and under	37
4 and under	48
5 and under	54
6 and under	58
7 and under	60

Percentage cumulative frequency table showing the new response rates

Response time	% Cumulative frequency
	0
1 and under	6.67
2 and under	30.00
3 and under	61.67
4 and under	80.00
5 and under	90.00
6 and under	96.67
7 and under	100.00

The response rates are now much faster – 80 per cent of all being 4 minutes or less. Most are between 2 and 3 minutes.

Activity 3

The histogram is shown in Figure SA9

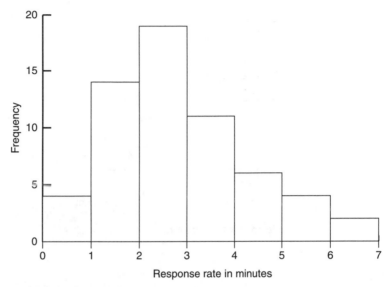

Figure SA9 New Help Line response times

Activity 4

Weight in kg	Frequency	Class size	Height of rectangle = frequency/class size
30 and under 50	40	20	2
50 and under 60	64	10	6.4
60 and under 65	80	5	16
65 and under 70	72	5	14.4
70 and under 80	48	10	4.8
80 and under 100	32	20	1.6

The histogram is shown in Figure SA10

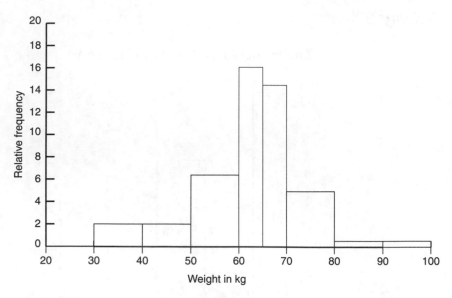

Figure SA10 Histogram to show weights

Activity 5

See Figures SA11 and SA12.

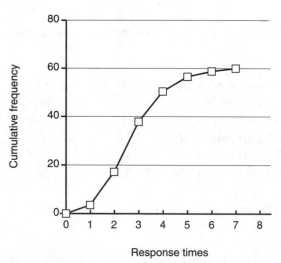

Figure SA11 Ogive for the new response times

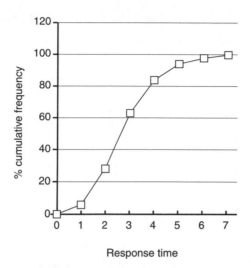

Figure SA12 The percentago cumulative frequency

Self-assessment

1. Multiple choice
1.1 (a)
1.2 (c)
1.3 (d)
1.4 (a)

2. Exercises
2.1 Bedding manufacturer

Spring pressure	Number of springs, f
1.30 and under 1.35	12
1.35 and under 1.40	34
1.40 and under 1.45	77
1.45 and under 1.50	145
1.50 and under 1.55	182
1.55 and under 1.60	171
1.60 and under 1.65	80
1.65 and under 1.70	39
1.70 and under 1.75	10
Total =	750

(a) The histogram is shown in Figure SA13.

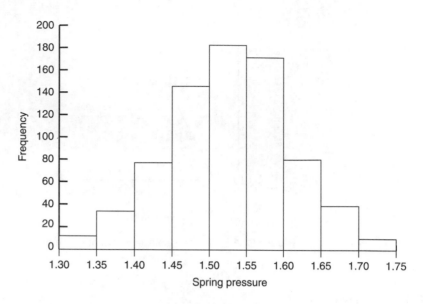

Figure SA13 Histogram to show spring pressure

(b) Cumulative frequency table

Pressure	Cumulative frequency
Under 1.3	0
Under 1.35	12
Under 1.4	46
Under 1.45	123
Under 1.5	268
Under 1.55	450
Under 1.6	621
Under 1.65	701
Under 1.7	740
Under 1.75	750

(c) The ogive is shown in Figure SA14.

(d) Number of springs = 498

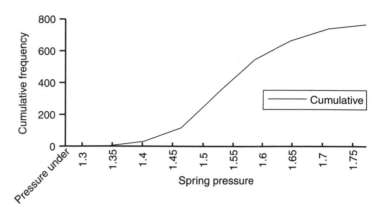

Figure SA14 Ogive showing spring pressure

2.2 Milk yield

Yield in litres	Number of cows	Class interval	Height
under 10	6	10	0.6
10 and under 12	10	2	5.00
12 and under 16	25	4	6.25
16 and under 20	32	4	8.00
20 and under 22	25	2	12.50
22 and under 24	28	2	14.00
24 and under 30	32	6	5.33
30 and under 34	40	4	10.00
34 and under 40	55	6	9.17
40 and under 50	12	10	1.20
Total =	265		

The histogram is shown in Figure SA15.

3. Ideas for the case study

Draw histograms and mark on the specification limits. For each supplier, check how many rivets fall outside these limits.

Construct frequency tables, cumulative frequency tables and percentage cumulative frequency tables for the times.

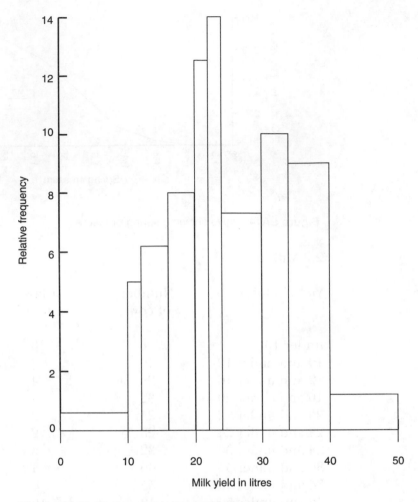

Figure SA15 Histogram to show milk yield

Chapter 6

Activity 1: 25.52 min; 680 cars; 38.7 min
Activity 2: 1.99 cartons; 13.93p
Activity 3: 21 min
Activity 4: Q1 = 17.4; Q3 = 35.3; 17.9
Acticity 5: 29.2
Activity 6: 1.41
Activity 7: 2.85; 1.45

Self-assessment

1. Multiple choice

1.1 (b)	1.5 (c)
1.2 (a)	1.6 (c)
1.3 (a)	1.7 (a)
1.4 (a)	1.8 (d)

2. Explain

2.1 Assumes data is evenly spread around mid-point, if this is not true then the statistics calculated from the frequency table will not be as accurate.

2.2 Calculations can be done more quickly.

2.3 When there are a few very large observations.

3. Exercises

3.1 (a) $x = 4$, $y = 6$; (b) 4

3.2 (a) Mean for 14 weeks = 34.14; (b) mean for last 8 weeks = 24.52

3.3 (a) 62.75; (b) 19.23; (c) 15

3.4 (a) 1.53; (b) Q1 = 1.49, Q3 = 1.58; (c) 0.09; (d) 1.5276 (e) 0.0806

4. Ideas for the case study

Find the summary statistics and determine, from the shape of the data, the most appropriate.

Chapter 7

Activity 1: (1) 0.24; (2) 0.28; (3) 0.32

Case Study Exercise 1

1. p(win) = 0.6

win contract and employ one more permanent researcher, and sub-contract when necessary = 0.204

win contract and employ two more permanent researchers, and sub-contract when necessary = 0.108

2. p(win) = 0.75

win contract and employ no more permanent researchers, and sub-contract when necessary = 0.51

win contract and employ one more permanent researcher, and sub-contract when necessary = 0.255
win contract and employ two more permanent researchers, and sub-contract when necessary = 0.135

Activity 2: 0.927
Activity 3: £1.50

Case Study Exercise 2

The cheapest option is to employ 13 permanent researchers, and subcontract when necessary.

Self-assessment

1. Multiple choice
1.1 (a) D; (b) F; (c) B; (d) H; (e) I
1.2 (d)

2. Explain the meaning of the following:
2.1 Two events are independent if the outcome of the first does not affect the outcome of the second.
2.2 Two events are mutually exclusive if they cannot occur together.
2.3 The conditional probability is the probability of one event happening, given that another event has already happened.
2.4 An expected value is the average value, or outcome, which would result over a long period of time.

3. Calculate the following probabilities:
3.1 0.65
3.2 (a) 0.05; (b) 0.6; (c) 0.4
3.3 (a) 0.7; (b) 0.3; (c) 0.441,
3.4 0.92
3.5 (a) 0.77; (b) 0.20; (c) 0.02

4. Ideas for case study
A probability tree will help you follow the process, 339 seeds are needed. Calculate the expected value of the profit for each option.

Chapter 8

Case Study Exercise 1: 103.53; 2.69
Case Study Exercise 2: all percentages are close to values of the normal distribution
Activity 1: (1) 0.1151; (2) 0.3849; (3) 0.9756; (4) 0.9452; (5) 0.0998
Activity 2: (a) 6680; (b) 4010; (c) 68 260
Case Study Exercise 3: 106.93

Self-assessment

1. Multiple choice
1.1 (b)
1.2 (b) and (d)
1.3 (a) and (b)
1.4 (b)

2. Use the normal distribution tables to find the probabilities:
(a) 0.1587; (b) 0.0218; (c) 0.1578; (d) 0.9032; (e) 0.042; (f) 0.8095;
(g) 0.1775

3. Use the normal distribution tables to find the value of x:
(a) 2.1973; (b) 2.0969; (c)1.8808; (d) 1.8522

4. A random variable follows a normal distribution with mean = 100 and standard deviation = 5, the probability:
(a) 0.1151; (b) 0.02275; (c) 0.0808; (d) 0.2743; (e) 0.4967

5. The number of times in the next 250 days that the post will arrive:
(a) 5.7; (b) 0.3; (c) 171.32

6. Percentage of batteries will not last for 45 hours of continuous use?
0.135 per cent

7. Ideas for case study
Find the percentage of output which meets the specification. Then find number scrapped, number meeting the specification, and the number too long, but can be cut.

Chapter 9

Case Study Exercise 1: $y = 4 + 3x$
Case Study Exercise 2: weather; operator; type of lorry; time of day etc.
Activity 1: yes, there does seem to be a linear relationship. Condition, make, model, demand.
Activity 2: (a) $y = 22.14 + 14.82x$; (b) 71.046 per cent
Activity 3: 0.916
Activity 4: 0.94 (a high correlation)
Case Study Exercise 3: 0.65

Self-assessment

1. Multiple choice

1.1 (c)   1.4 (c)
1.2 (d)   1.5 (a)
1.3 (c)

2. Briefly explain the following:

2.1 A scatter diagram. Plot of the points x and y, used to determine whether the data exhibits any obvious pattern

2.2 The objectives of regression analysis. To find the equation linking the two variables

2.3 The dependent variable. If the two variables are correlated, it is the variable whose values we are trying to predict. It depends on the independent variable.

2.4 The independent variable. This is the predictor variable

2.5 The slope of the regression line. The slope is the increase in the dependent variable for unit increase in the independent variable.

2.6 The y intercept. The value of the dependent variable when the independent variable = 0.

2.7 A positive correlation. As the independent variable increases, so does the dependent variable.

2.8 A zero correlation. There is no relationship between the two variables.

2.9 A rank correlation. The correlation which is found from two sets of rankings, rather than two sets of measurements.

2.10 These are mathematical measures. They do not prove that one variable causes another to happen.

3. Problems to solve
3.1 (b)(i) Sales = 209.4 + 5.5 × advertising expenditure;
(ii) $r = 0.973$; (iii) Jan 1999 = 369; Feb 1999 = 330.5

3.2 $r = 0.9276$, a high correlation

3.3 (a) Demand = 53.56 − 1.77 × price; (b) $r = -0.902$

3.4 $r = 0.5061$, no correlation between test rankings and manager's preference

4. Ideas for the case studies
4.1 MUFTI furniture
The overhead cost is the dependent variable. There are three possible independent variables: direct labour, number of flat packs and cardboard. Plot a scatter diagram for each in turn. If any appears to show a correlation, find its value and the associated regression equation.

4.2 Miss Smith
The error rate is the dependent variable. There are three possible independent variables. Plot a scatter diagram for each in turn. If any appears to show a correlation, use the pre-programmed correlation coefficient to find its value.

Chapter 10

Activity 1

(1) Q1 = 27.82; Q2 = 2.51; Q3 = −23.84; Q4 = −6.49
(2) Forecasts: Q1 = 86.16; Q2 = 61.91; Q3 = 36.64; Q4 = 55.05

Self-assessment

1. Forecasting
1.1 Forecasting helps business to plan for the future.
1.2(a) Long-term trend, cyclical components, seasonal variation and random variation
(b) Short-term trend, seasonal variation and random variation

2.1 Petrol sales

(b) Three-point cycle.

(c) Week 2 to week 11

203.33, 216.67, 226.67, 230.00, 233.33, 236.67, 243.33, 250.00, 253.33, 253.33

2.2 PC sales

(c) Q1 = –0.44; Q2 = –1.07; Q3 = 0.59; Q4 = 0.92

(d) Forecasts: Q1 = 7.21; Q2 = 6.77; Q3 = 8.61; Q4 = 9.13

3. Ideas for the case study

Plot out the monthly data to determine the pattern. Use this pattern to from the basis of your forecasting model.

Glossary of terms

Symbol	Pronunciation	Formula (if applicable)	Meaning
x			One of the most common letters used to represent an unknown or a variable. In regression analysis it is the independent variable
y			Another of the most common letters used to represent an unknown or a variable. In regression analysis it is the dependent variable
f			The frequency, which is the number of times a variable takes one particular value
n			The number of items in the sample
N			The number of items in the population
Σ	sigma (This is the upper case sigma)		Add up
Σx	sigma x		Add up the values of x
Σf	sigma f		Add up the values of f
$\bar{x}$	x bar	$\Sigma x / n$ or $\Sigma fx / Sf$	The sample mean

Symbol	Pronunciation	Formula	Meaning
μ	mu	$\Sigma x/N$ or $\Sigma fx/\Sigma f$	The population mean
s		$\sqrt{\Sigma(x-\bar{x})^2/n}$ or $\sqrt{\dfrac{\Sigma fx^2}{\Sigma f} - (\bar{x}^2)}$	The sample standard deviation (Sometimes $\Sigma(x-x)^2$ is divided by $n-1$)
σ	Sigma (This is the lower case sigma) or	$\sqrt{\dfrac{\Sigma(x-\bar{x})^2}{N}}$ $\sqrt{(\Sigma fx^2/\Sigma f) - (\bar{x}^2)}$	The population standard deviation
b		$\dfrac{\Sigma xy - n\,\bar{x}\bar{y}}{\Sigma x^2 - n\,\bar{x}^2}$	The slope of the regression line
a		$\bar{y} - b\,\bar{x}$	The intercept of the regression line
r		$\dfrac{\Sigma xy - n\,\bar{x}\,\bar{y}}{\sqrt{(\Sigma x^2 - n\bar{x}^2)(\Sigma y^2 - n\bar{y}^2)}}$	Pearson's product moment correlation coefficient
R_{rank}		$1 - \dfrac{6\Sigma d^2}{n(n^2-1)}$	Spearman's rank correlation coefficient
p_0			Base year price
p_n			Current price
q_0			Quantity bought in base year
q_n			Quantity bought in current year

Appendix A

Areas in the tail of the normal distribution

The table gives the area under one tail of the normal distribution curve.

$z = \frac{(x - \mu)}{\sigma}$	.00	.01	.02	.03	.04	.05	.06	.07	.08	.09
0.0	.5000	.4960	.4920	.4880	.4840	.4801	.4761	.4721	.4681	.4641
0.1	.4602	.4562	.4522	.4483	.4443	.4404	.4364	.4325	.4286	.4247
0.2	.4207	.4168	.4129	.4090	.4052	.4013	.3974	.3936	.3897	.3859
0.3	.3821	.3783	.3745	.3707	.3669	.3632	.3594	.3557	.3520	.3483
0.4 ·	.3446	.3409	.3372	.3336	.3300	.3264	.3228	.3192	.3156	.3121
0.5	.3085	.3050	.3015	.2981	.2946	.2912	.2877	.2843	.2810	.2776
0.6	.2743	.2709	.2676	.2643	.2611	.2578	.2546	.2514	.2483	.2451
0.7	.2420	.2389	.2358	.2327	.2296	.2266	.2236	.2206	.2177	.2148
0.8	.2119	.2090	.2061	.2033	.2005	.1977	.1949	.1922	.1894	.1867
0.9	.1841	.1814	.1788	.1762	.1736	.1711	.1685	.1660	.1635	.1611
1.0	.1587	.1562	.1539	.1515	.1492	.1469	.1446	.1423	.1401	.1379
1.1	.1357	.1335	.1314	.1292	.1271	.1251	.1230	.1210	.1190	.1170
1.2	.1151	.1131	.1112	.1093	.1075	.1056	.1038	.1020	.1003	.0985
1.3	.0968	.0951	.0934	.0918	.0901	.0885	.0869	.0853	.0838	.0823
1.4	.0808	.0793	.0778	.0764	.0749	.0735	.0721	.0708	.0694	.0681

(*continued*)

$z = \dfrac{(x - \mu)}{\sigma}$	.00	.01	.02	.03	.04	.05	.06	.07	.08	.09
1.5	.0668	.0655	.0643	.0630	.0618	.0606	.0594	.0582	.0571	.0559
1.6	.0548	.0537	.0526	.0516	.0505	.0495	.0485	.0475	.0465	.0455
1.7	.0446	.0436	.0427	.0418	.0409	.0401	.0392	.0384	.0375	.0367
1.8	.0359	.0351	.0344	.0336	.0329	.0322	.0314	.0307	.0301	.0294
1.9	.0287	.0281	.0274	.0268	.0262	.0256	.0250	.0244	.0239	.0233
2.0	.02275	.02222	.02169	.02118	.02608	.02018	.01970	.01923	.01876	.01831
2.1	.01786	.01743	.01700	.01659	.01618	.01578	.01539	.01500	.01463	.01426
2.2	.01390	.01355	.01321	.01287	.01255	.01222	.01191	.01160	.01130	.01101
2.3	.01072	.01044	.01017	.00990	.00964	.00939	.00914	.00889	.00866	.00842
2.4	.00820	.00798	.00776	.00755	.00734	.00714	.00695	.00676	.00657	.00639
2.5	.00621	.00604	.00587	.00570	.00554	.00539	.00523	.00508	.00494	.00480
2.6	.00466	.00453	.00440	.00427	.00415	.00402	.00391	.00379	.00368	.00357
2.7	.00347	.00336	.00326	.00317	.00307	.00298	.00289	.00280	.00272	.00264
2.8	.00256	.00248	.00240	.00233	.00226	.00219	.00212	.00205	.00199	.00193
2.9	.00187	.00181	.00175	.00169	.00164	.00159	.00154	.00149	.00144	.00139
3.0	.00135									
3.1	.00097									
3.2	.00069									
3.3	.00048									
3.4	.00034									
3.5	.00023									
3.6	.00016									
3.7	.00011									
3.8	.00007									
3.9	.00005									
4.0	.00003									

This table is based on Table 3 of *Statistical Tables for Science, Engineering, Management and Business Studies* (4th edition) by Murdock and Murdock (1998) published by Macmillan Press Ltd. Reproduced by kind permission of the authors and publishers.

Appendix B

Percentage points of the normal distribution

The table gives the value of z corresponding to an area A under one tail of the normal distribution curve.

A	Z	A	Z	A	Z	A	Z	A	Z	A	Z
.50	0.0000	.050	1.6449	.030	1.8808	.020	2.0537	.010	2.3263	.050	1.6449
.45	0.1257	.048	1.6646	.029	1.8957	.019	2.0749	.009	2.3656	.010	2.3263
.40	0.2533	.046	1.6849	.028	1.9110	.018	2.0969	.008	2.4089	.001	3.0902
.35	0.3853	.044	1.7060	.027	1.9268	.017	2.1201	.007	2.4573	.0001	3.7190
.30	0.5244	.042	1.7279	.026	1.9431	.016	2.1444	.006	2.5121	.00001	4.2649
.25	0.6745	.040	1.7507	.025	1.9600	.015	2.1701	.005	2.5758	.025	1.9600
.20	0.8416	.038	1.7744	.024	1.9774	.014	2.1973	.004	2.6521	.005	2.5758
.15	1.0364	.036	1.7991	.023	1.9954	.013	2.2262	.003	2.7478	.0005	3.2905
.10	1.2816	.034	1.8250	.022	2.0141	.012	2.2571	.002	2.8782	.00005	3.8906
.05	1.6449	.032	1.8522	.021	2.0335	.011	2.2904	.001	3.0902	.000005	4.4172

This table is based on Table 4 of *Statistical Tables for Science, Engineering, Management and Business Studies* (4th edition) by Murdock and Murdock (1998) published by Macmillan Press Ltd. Reproduced by kind permission of the authors and publishers.

Index

A priori probability, 146, 148
Arithmetic mean *see* Mean
Arithmetic progressions, 26
Average, 114, 119, 125, 126, 128, 140, 192
Axes, 17, 101, 106

Bar charts, 76–7
Base period, 37, 38
Base weighting, 39, 41

Charts, 75–86
Classes, 94, 99, 104, 162
Cluster sampling, 62
Common difference, 26, 27
Common ratio, 28
Component bar chart, 77–8, 87
Compound interest, 28–30
Conditional probability, 156
Continuous data, 54, 97, 102
Correlation, 191, 203–14, 222
Correlation coefficient, 203–8, 214
Cumulative frequency curve *see* Ogive
Cumulative frequency table, 99–101, 106,
    108, 115, 116, 129
Current weighting, 39, 42, 44

Decimals, 3, 5, 6, 7
Decision theory, 163
Dependent variable, 193, 194, 214, 222
Depreciation, 26–7, 28, 30
Descriptive classes, 51–2
Desk research, 65
Deviation from the mean, 131
Discrete data, 54, 97, 101
Dispersion, 128

Equations, 15, 17, 214
Event, 146, 147, 157
Expected value, 159–63
Experimentation, 64

Family expenditure survey, 37
Focus group, 53
Forecasting, 234–41
Forecasting techniques, 221–41
Frequency, 94, 97, 102, 104, 115, 134, 161
Frequency table, 92–9, 101, 108, 116, 120,
    122, 125, 134, 147, 161, 168, 169

General index of retail prices, 37–8, 44, 45
Geometric progressions, 28–9
Graphs, 17–9, 69, 75, 84

Histogram, 101–6, 108, 169, 170, 172

Independent variable, 193, 194, 214, 222
Index numbers, 36–45, 45
Intercept, 20–1, 197, 202, 214
Interquartile range, 129–30, 140

Laspeyre price index, 39–41
Least squares regression *see* Regression
Linear regression *see* Regression
Long-term forecasting, 223–5

Mean, 119–24, 128, 132, 140, 161, 162,
    168, 171, 172, 177, 184, 186
Mean deviation, 132
Measurements, 54, 92, 168, 186
Measures of location, 114–28
Measures of variation, 128–39

Median, 114–18, 129, 130, 140, 168
Mid point, 122, 123, 162
Mode, 119, 140, 168
Moving average, 227–32, 241
Moving total, 227, 229
Multiple bar chart, 77, 87
Multiple regression, 214
Mutually exclusive events, 151
Mystery shopper, 64

Negative numbers, 3, 4
Net present value, 34–5
Normal distribution, 168–87
Normal distribution curve, 170–3
Normal distribution tables, 173–86

Observation, 64
Ogive, 106–8, 129, 130
Ordered classes, 52, 53
Ordinal numbers, 52

Paasche price index, 42–4
Pearson's product moment correlation
    coefficient, 204, 207, 209, 212
Percentage component bar chart, 77–8,
    87
Percentage cumulative frequency, 100,
    108
Percentages, 9–11, 73
Pie charts, 79–81, 87
Population, 50, 53, 57–8, 60, 61, 62, 119
Population mean, 119
Population standard deviation, 134
Positive numbers, 3, 4
Powers, 13–14, 33
Present value, 31–6
Price relative index numbers, 37–8
Primary data, 55, 56, 63, 65
Probability, 146–63, 172, 173
Probability distribution, 161, 168, 186
Probability tree, 157–58
Progressions, 25–31
Proportions, 9–11

Qualitative data, 57
Quantitative data, 50, 51
Quarterly variation, 228, 233
Quartile, 129–30
Questioning, 64–5
Questionnaire, 64–5
Quota sampling, 63

Random error, 192–203
Random numbers, 58, 62
Random variation, 224, 225, 226, 232, 241
Range, 128–9
Rank correlation, 209–14
Rankings, 52, 209, 212
Raw data, 68, 120
Regression, 191, 196, 197–203, 227
Relative frequency, 148, 156, 162
Rounding, 8

Sample, 50, 53, 57–8, 61, 62, 63, 119, 134
Sample mean, 119
Sample standard deviation, 134
Sampling fraction, 60, 61
Sampling frame, 58, 61, 62
Scatter diagram, 194, 195, 196, 200, 209,
    214, 222, 223
Seasonal variation, 222, 225, 226, 227,
    228, 229, 232–4, 241
Secondary data, 55–6, 65
Short-term forecasting, 225–6
Significant figures, 8–9
Simple bar chart, 76, 87
Simple interest, 26, 28, 32
Simple random sampling, 58–60
Slope, 20–1, 197, 201, 214
Spearman's rank correlation coefficient,
    209–14
Standard deviation, 130–9, 140, 168, 171,
    172, 177, 184, 186
Standard Normal distribution, 173–80
Straight line, 20–1, 191, 192, 200, 203
Stratified sampling, 60–1, 63
Survey methods, 63–5

Systematic sampling, 60

Tables, 71–5
Time series analysis, 222–41
Trend, 222, 224, 225, 226, 227–32, 234, 241

Variables, 5, 15, 54, 92, 94, 173, 191, 203
Variance, 132

Z charts, 81–6
Z statistic, 173–86

Tutor Support material is available....

A free lecturer's supplement containing:

♦ *Guidelines*
♦ *Model answers*
♦ *Solutions to activities*
♦ *Ideas for development of case studies*

is also vailable either as **hard copy** or is **downloadable from the BH website (password protected)** from Autumn 1999.

To order a **Tutor Resource Pack for Quantitative Methods**, please contact our Management Marketing Department, quoting **ISBN 07506 4513X**, on:

Tel: 01865 314477
Fax: 01865 314455
E-mail: bhmarketing@repp.co.uk